PRACTICAL QABALAH MAGICK

OTHER BOOKS BY THESE AUTHORS

BY SORITA D'ESTE & DAVID RANKINE

HEKATE LIMINAL RITES

THE ISLES OF THE MANY GODS

VISIONS OF THE CAILLEACH

THE GUISES OF THE MORRIGAN

PRACTICAL ELEMENTAL MAGICK

PRACTICAL PLANETARY MAGICK

CIRCLE OF FIRE

WICCA MAGICKAL BEGINNINGS

BY SORITA D'ESTE

ARTEMIS – VIRGIN GODDESS OF THE SUN & MOON

TOWARDS THE WICCAN CIRCLE

HEKATE KEYS TO THE CROSSROADS (EDITOR)

PRIESTESSES PYTHONESSES & SIBYLS (EDITOR)

HORNS OF POWER (EDITOR)

BOTH SIDES OF HEAVEN (EDITOR)

BY DAVID RANKINE

THE BOOK OF TREASURE SPIRITS

BECOMING MAGICK

CLIMBING THE TREE OF LIFE

CRYSTALS HEALING & FOLKLORE

HEKA ANCIENT EGYPTIAN MAGIC & RITUAL

BY DAVID RANKINE, WITH STEPHEN SKINNER

A COLLECTION OF MAGICAL SECRETS

PRACTICAL ANGEL MAGIC OF DR JOHN DEE'S ENOCHIAN TABLES

KEYS TO THE GATEWAY OF MAGIC

THE GOETIA OF DR RUDD

THE VERITABLE KEY OF SOLOMON

THE GRIMOIRE OF ST CYPRIAN – CLAVIS INFERNI

ABOUT THE AUTHORS

Sorita d'Este and David Rankine are esoteric authors, occult researchers and magicians who bring their knowledge of the wisdom of the ancient world into the modern age. They combine their knowledge of a diverse range of occult subjects and their experience of different traditions to create new and fresh ritual material, based on source material research.

Their work is firmly rooted in tradition, whilst pushing the boundaries beyond the accepted status quo to expand the spectrum of available techniques and knowledge. Their books have covered such subjects as the magic, mysteries and Gods and Goddesses of Ancient Egypt, Greece, Rome, Celtic Britain and Ireland, as well as the Qabalah, ceremonial magic, angels, demons and grimoires.

Today they live in Wales, near the eccentric book town capital of the world Hay-on-Wye.

For more information see:

www.sorita.co.uk

www.ritualmagick.co.uk

You can also write the authors:

Sorita d'Este & David Rankine

c/o BM Avalonia

London

WC1N 3XX

United Kingdom

Published by Avalonia

BM Avalonia
London
WC1N 3XX
England, UK

www.avaloniabooks.co.uk
www.avaloniabooks.com

PRACTICAL QABALAH MAGICK
Copyright © Sorita and David Rankine 2009

ISBN-10: 1-905297-22-X
ISBN-13: 978-1-905297-22-1

First Edition, October 2009
Design by Satori
Jacket design by Io Lig © 2009

British Library Cataloguing in Publication Data. A catalogue record for
this book is available from the British Library

PRACTICAL

QABALAH

MAGICK

WORKING THE MAGICK OF THE PRACTICAL QABALAH
AND THE TREE OF LIFE IN THE WESTERN MYSTERY TRADITION

DAVID RANKINE & SORITA D'ESTE

PUBLISHED BY AVALONIA 2009

"If you want to single yourself out in the world so that the secrets of the world and the mysteries of wisdom should be revealed to you, study this Misnah [work] and be careful about it till the day of your passing.
Do not try to understand what lies behind you and do investigate the words of your lips. You should try to understand what is in your heart and keep silent, so that you will be worthy of the beauty of the Merkavah [chariot of God]."

HEKHALOT ZUTARTI (THE LESSER PALACES) C3RD-C8TH.

Contents

CONTEMPLATIONS 78

THE VIBRATORY FORMULA 87

THE DIVINE NAMES 91

UNIFICATION OF THE DIVINE NAMES 94

THE ARCHANGELS 99

APPENDIXES

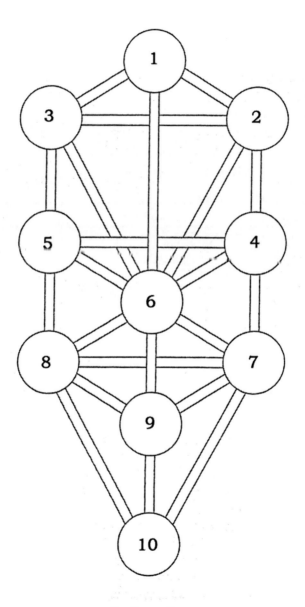

THE TREE OF LIFE

CHAPTER 1

Qabalah Magick

"Powers of the Kingdom, be beneath my left foot, and within my right hand. Glory and Eternity touch my shoulders, and guide me in the Paths of Victory. Mercy and Justice be ye the Equilibrium and Splendour of my life. Understanding and Wisdom give unto me the Crown. Spirits of Malkuth conduct me between the two columns whereon is supported the whole edifice of the Temple. Angels of Netzach and of Hod strengthen me upon the Cubical Stone of Yesod."[1]

The Qabalah gives understanding and wisdom through knowledge, strength and mercy through beauty, and a foundation of victory and splendour, crowning the seeker within their own kingdom and raising them to the heights of their own genius. Qabalah is an experiential path which lives up to its literal meaning of *'received wisdom'*, gained as the seeker travels through the worlds guided by the Tree of Life, attaining knowledge and understanding.

As we know it today, the Qabalah, as found in the Western Mystery Tradition, is a system of magical philosophy and spiritual practice which syncretised components of Gnosticism, Neo-Platonism, and early Jewish mysticism with aspects of ancient Sumerian and Egyptian cosmologies. In Europe, during the twelfth to fourteenth centuries these diverse sources flowed together into a melting pot of spiritual and magical ideologies generating a lucid, coherent and practical path of spiritual realisation. The resulting philosophies and

---

[1] The Qabalistic Invocation of Solomon, Eliphas Levi.

practices would subsequently influence and inspire a wide range of magical and spiritual traditions which in turn would be highly influential on the western mystery traditions of alchemy, hermeticism, Freemasonry, Rosicrucianism and all their many derivatives. The influence of the Qabalah can be seen in nearly all the major magical books from the Renaissance, including the *Key of Solomon*, the *Heptameron*, Agrippa's *Three Books of Occult Philosophy* and Kircher's *Oedipus Aegypticus*.

Juxtaposed with the emergence of Qabalah as a prominent philosophy, came its distilled essence in the glyph known as *Otz Chiim* ('*the Tree of Life*'). Reflecting the commonly used scale of ten numbers combined with the twenty-two Hebrew letters, the image of the Tree of Life comprises the ten Sephiroth ('*emanations*'), which are connected by twenty-two horizontal, vertical and diagonal paths. These Sephiroth and Paths weave together the symbolism of the four elements, the seven classical planets, and the zodiac as a single articulate whole. This coalesces all the key elements of the western mystery traditions since its earliest emergence through to the modern day.

The wide spectrum of practices and principles of the Qabalah can be seen as an ever-expanding panoramic horizon, with your own individual view being expanded to infinity through your experiences and the realisations they bring. This expansion of ideas with perspective can be demonstrated by the idea of the Four Worlds and how they relate to both the division of the Tree of Life, and also to the powers of each individual Sephira.

On one level, each Sephira is said to exist in all Four Worlds, which correspond to its Divine Name, archangel, order of angels and heaven, representing different levels of manifestation of the creative essence. Yet on another level the Four Worlds divide the Sephiroth into triads down the Tree of Life based on the principle of force and form balanced in action or repose, with each World containing three of the Sephiroth (with the fourth World only containing the final Sephira of Malkuth).

The ability of the Qabalah to permutate and present different valid perceptions of the same ideologies makes it an extremely powerful system for creating change on many levels. This is essential to its adaptability and versatility, with its principles applying through the Worlds. In other words, when incorporating it into your life, it should permeate not only your spiritual life, but also the way you live your mental, emotional and material lives and the decisions you make throughout.

The practices in this book contain elements of the twin threads of early Qabalah, that of the schools of *Maaseh Bereshith* (*'Workings of the Beginning'*) and *Maaseh Merkavah* (*'Workings of the Chariot'*). The school of *Maaseh Bereshith* was focused around the cosmology and cosmogony of the first chapter of the book of Genesis as a revelatory text; whilst that of *Maaseh Merkavah* focused on the first chapter of the book of Ezekiel as the inspiration for the active mystical ascent of the Tree of Life into the presence of God. Both of these schools have influenced the modern forms of Qabalah, with the emphasis moving perhaps more towards *Maaseh Bereshith*, and away from the more radical and dramatic path of the Merkavah Rider, seeking to enter the throne room of God. We have endeavoured to restore the balance, and blend material drawn from and inspired by both paths to provide practices and philosophies which encompass the magic of the whole of the Tree of Life in all its glory.

The work of scholars such as Gershom Scholem, Aryeh Kaplan and Moshe Idel which has been published in recent decades has greatly expanded the field of available Qabalistic source works. The work of these authors and their successors has resulted in an improved range of accessible scholarly works on many different aspects of the Qabalah, including the Merkavah tradition. Likewise, the works of the great Jewish medieval and Renaissance Qabalists such as Abraham Abulafia,

Moses Cordevero, Moses de Leon and Elaihu Gaon have become more easily available. This increase in accessibility also applies to Christian Qabalists of the Renaissance such as Pico della Mirandola, Johannes Reuchlin and Athansius Kircher, whose work channelled the Qabalah into the mainstream of the Western Esoteric traditions. By illustrating the principles with information from older Qabalistic texts, we demonstrate the unbroken continuity and immense value of the Qabalistic tradition. At the same time we have included practices which we have developed as a result of decades of work with the Qabalah, showing how you can evolve effective new techniques through a solid foundation in the principles.

Bearing this in mind, the reader will find that the material presented in this volume is at times very different to that of modern magical Qabalah as taught by those influenced by the Golden Dawn, a Victorian magical society whose work has subsequently been very influential on the philosophies found in the Western Mystery Tradition since the early 20th century. Whilst we are familiar with their teachings and at times draw from it, our own research and inspiration comes from earlier sources. Our approach was directed in this way through the research we have been conducting into the diverse areas of the history of magical practice in different historical and cultural settings. Many of the sources we drew upon would have been unavailable to, or otherwise unfamiliar to, the founders of the Golden Dawn and their disciples, and as a result the corpus of material they use can at times be restricted. By taking this modern and holistic approach we are able to provide a system which is in keeping with the earlier western magical traditions, and which provides a wider scope for study, understanding and practice.

Table of Intentions

Intention	Sephira
Adaptability, developing	Hod
Ambition, development of	Chesed
Anger, controlling	Geburah
Astral Travel	Yesod
Attraction, increasing	Netzach
Beauty, developing	Netzach
Birth, safely	Yesod, Malkuth
Boundaries, strengthening	Tiphereth
Business success	Hod
Career success	Chesed, Tiphereth
Change, encouraging/accepting	Malkuth
Clairvoyance, developing	Yesod
Communication, improving	Hod
Compassion, increasing	Chesed
Courage, enhancing	Geburah
Creativity, increasing	Netzach
Cynicism, overcoming	Binah
Discord, causing	Geburah
Discord, preventing	Hod
Dreams, promoting & remembering	Yesod
Duty, performing	Binah
Ego, controlling	Netzach, Chesed
Energy, increasing	Geburah, Tiphereth
Enthusiasm, increasing	Chesed
Equilibrium, establishing	Binah
Ethics, developing	Chesed
Examination study	Binah
Examination success	Hod
Fear, dispelling	Geburah
Fertility, increasing	Netzach
Flexibility, developing	Hod
Fortune, improving	Chesed
Friendship, developing	Netzach, Malkuth
Future, learning the	Yesod, Hod
Glamour, developing	Yesod
Harmony, developing	Tiphereth, Chokmah
Healing, giving	Tiphereth, Hod

Health, improving	Chesed, Tiphereth
Home, protecting	Binah, Malkuth
Honour, acquiring	Chesed
Humour, improving	Chesed
Illusions, creating	Yesod
Illusions, dispelling	Binah, Malkuth
Influence, developing	Hod
Intimacy, accepting	Yesod
Journey, protection	Hod (air); Yesod (sea) ; Malkuth (land)
Knowledge, increasing	Hod
Law, dealing with	Binah, Chesed
Leadership/assertiveness, developing	Chesed, Tiphereth
Love, obtaining or promoting	Netzach
Luck, improving	Chesed
Lust, satisfying	Netzach, Geburah
Memory, improving	Hod
Money, acquiring	Tiphereth
Motivation, increasing	Tiphereth
Music, learning or improving	Hod
Passion, increasing	Netzach, Geburah
Patience, developing	Binah
Patronage, obtaining	Tiphereth, Chesed
Peace, establishing	Tiphereth, Hod
Pleasure, ensuring	Netzach
Practicality, developing	Binah
Pride, dispelling	Chesed
Promotion, gaining	Chesed, Tiphereth
Property, recovering	Hod
Public speaking, successfully	Hod
Responsibility, taking	Chesed
Self-confidence, increasing	Netzach
Self-confidence, developing	Binah
Sex-drive, decreasing	Binah
Sex-drive, increasing	Geburah
Social skills, improving	Netzach
Strength, increasing	Geburah
Teaching, developing	Binah
Truth, learning or promoting	Chesed
Unconscious, accessing	Yesod
Vigour, increasing	Geburah
Wealth, improving	Chesed, Tiphereth
Willpower, strengthening	Tiphereth

The Hebrew Letters and their Correspondences

Letter	Attribute	Colour	Life Influence	Day	Direction
The Mother Letters					
Shin	Fire	Glowing Red	Goals	Any	Up
Aleph	Air	Bright Yellow	Communication	Any	Centre
Mem	Water	Deep Blue	Emotions	Any	Down
The Double Letters					
Beth	Mercury	Orange	Wisdom	Wednesday	South
Gimel	Moon	Violet	Wealth	Monday	North
Daleth	Venus	Emerald Green	Seed	Friday	East
Kaph	Jupiter	Royal Blue	Life	Thursday	Up
Peh	Mars	Scarlet Red	Dominance	Tuesday	Down
Resh	Sun	Yellow	Peace	Sunday	West
Tav	Saturn	Indigo	Grace	Saturday	Centre
The Single Letters					
Heh	Aries	Red	Speech	Tuesday	East Up
Vav	Taurus	Red-Orange	Thought	Friday	North East
Zayin	Gemini	Orange	Motion	Wednesday	East Down
Cheth	Cancer	Orange-Yellow	Sight	Monday	South Up
Teth	Leo	Yellow	Hearing	Sunday	South East
Yod	Virgo	Yellow-Green	Action	Wednesday	South Down
Lamed	Libra	Green	Coition	Friday	West Up
Nun	Scorpio	Green-Blue	Smell	Tuesday	South West
Samekh	Sagittarius	Blue	Sleep	Thursday	West Down
Ayin	Capricorn	Blue-Violet	Anger	Saturday	North Up
Tzaddi	Aquarius	Violet	Taste	Saturday	North West
Qoph	Pisces	Violet-Red	Laughter	Thursday	North Down

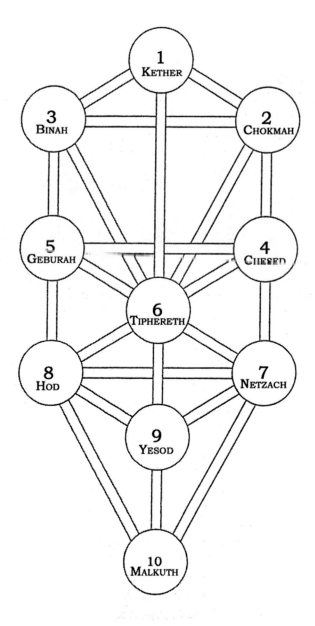

THE SEPHIROTH OF THE TREE OF LIFE

CHAPTER 2

The Sephiroth

"The most Ancient One is at the same time the most Hidden of the hidden . . . He made ten lights spring forth from his midst, lights which shine with the form which they have borrowed from Him."[2]

The Sephiroth are ten successive emanations from the divine which represent creation as the descent of pure spirit to matter through levels of manifestation. Sephiroth (singular, *Sephira*) means *'emanations'*, and comes from the same root as the words *Sepher* (meaning *'book'*), *Sephar* (meaning *'number'*) and *Sippur* (meaning *'communication'*). This is why the opening verse of the first great Qabalistic work, the *Sepher Yetzirah* includes the words:

> *"And He created His universe with three books [sepharim], with text [Sepher], with number [sephar] and with communication [sippur]."*[3]

Thus the Sephiroth can be perceived as being:

- Emanations of the different varieties of divine light – the colours of magick;
- Collections of knowledge and information about the different aspects of the divine – the books of magick;

---

[2] *Zohar.*

[3] *Sepher Yetzirah 1:1.*

- Numerations of the manifestations of the divine which enable the ordering of time and space through sequence and numerical relationship – the numbers of magick
- Communicated expressions of the divine – the words of magick.

The Sephiroth correspond to a huge range of symbols, from planets, parts of the human body to gods and to plants. This use as a symbolic map makes the Tree of Life an ideal cross-referencing tool, though this is only one of its many uses. The Sephiroth also represent states of being and knowing, and as your understanding of Qabalah grows, what each Sephira means to you will also change and grow.

There has been a great deal of debate about the origins of the Qabalah, fuelled by its early oral origins (being *received wisdom*). However, we do know that the first known written reference to the ten Sephiroth has been dated to around 70 CE in the early Talmud (Rabbinical religious, legal and ethical lore) in *Haggigah 12a*, where some of the Sephirothic names were already recorded.

> "Ten agencies through which God created the world, vis, wisdom, insight, cognition, strength, power, inexorableness, justice, right, lore, mercy."[4]

Although the names used for the Sephiroth have become standardised, in the past some of them had alternative names, which also provide insights into their nature. Popular examples of this are the names Gedulah (*'Glory'*) for Chesed and Pachad (*'Fear'*) and Din (*'Justice'*) for Geburah.

The date of 70 CE is also one commonly given for the *Sepher Yetzirah* (*'Book of Formation'*), one of the great Qabalistic source texts.

---

[4] *Haggigah 12a*, Talmud.

22 | Practical Qabalah Magick

This work is now generally acknowledged as being first or second century CE.

It has been suggested that the Qabalah was created much later, in the early Middle Ages, spreading across Europe with the publication of the other great source texts of the *Zohar* (1290) and the *Bahir* (1310) in the late thirteenth and early fourteenth century.

However when we consider that a relevant contextual reference from 386 CE is found in St Jerome's (347-420 CE) *Letter to Marcella XXV*, it is clear that this was not the case. St Jerome made reference to the ten Divine Names found in Scripture, which are essentially early versions of the Divine Names attributed to the Sephiroth. Jerome was an accomplished linguist, fluent in Greek, Hebrew and Latin, and is best known as the translator of the Latin Vulgate Bible. This reference suggests at least knowledge of the existence of the Qabalah, or its roots.

What we may agree is that the Qabalah, from roots which stretch back through ancient Sumeria and Egypt, growing into early Jewish mysticism, blossomed in the early Middle Ages in Europe (particularly in Spain and Italy) and spread the fruit which had been many centuries ripening through the minds of many great philosophers and magicians, rabbis and priests. This fruit of knowledge was also cross-fertilised by exposure to other great philosophical fruits, such as Gnosticism, Neo-Platonism and hermeticism.

Sephira	Meaning	Number	Position	World
Kether	Crown	1	First row, middle pillar	Atziluth
Chokmah	Wisdom	2	Second row, left pillar	Atziluth
Binah	Understanding	3	Second row, right pillar	Atziluth
Chesed	Mercy	4	Third row, left pillar	Briah

Geburah	Strength	5	Third row, right pillar	Briah
Tiphereth	Beauty	6	Fourth row, middle pillar	Briah
Netzach	Victory	7	Fifth row, left pillar	Yetzirah
Hod	Splendour	8	Fifth row, right pillar	Yetzirah
Yesod	Foundation	9	Sixth row, middle pillar	Yetzirah
Malkuth	Kingdom	10	Seventh row, middle pillar	Assiah

Kether (KThR)

"The countenance of His face is like the image of a spirit, like the form of a soul that no creature can recognise. His body is like chrysolith, filling the entire world. Neither the near nor the far can look at him."[5]

Sephira	Kether (Crown)
Number	1
Colour	White
Divine Name	AHIH (Eheieh)
Archangel	Metatron
Order of Angels	Chaioth ha-Qadosh (Holy Living Creatures), or Seraphim
Heaven	Rashith ha-Gilgalim (First Swirlings)
Body	Crown of the Head
Fragrance	Almond, Ambergris
Virtues	Completion of the Great Work
Vices	-

Kether (pronounced *Ket-er*, and meaning *Crown*) is the unknowable divine, the creative essence of life which cannot be represented, the template for all being. It is the first emanation from the limitless veils of unmanifest potential expressed as the three Veils of Negativity. Kether

---

[5] *Hekhalot Zutarti*, 356.

is equated with the First Swirlings, and in this sense can be seen as representing the Big Bang, the moment of creation when potential was first realised into manifestation.

As the template of creation, Kether contains within itself the plan of the entire Tree of Life. All the Sephiroth exist within Kether in potential, undivided and unexpressed, in a harmony of unity which is expressed through their emanation. This is why the *Zohar* describes Kether as *"the principle of all principles, the Secret Wisdom, the Most Exalted Crown, with which all Crowns and diadems are adorned."*

As the crown, it is worn at the top of the head, the highest point that can be achieved in a person. It thus represents the Divine Thought and the Most High, both of which are titles attributed to Kether. The crown represents the divine influence from above (the three Veils), and for this reason magicians and priests through the centuries have commonly worn headgear to either channel divine energy or protect themselves from it!

The magical formula of Kether is ARARITA; this is Notariqon (an acronym) for the phrase *Achad Resh Achudohtoh Resh Yechidotoh Temurahtoh Resh*, which translates as *"One is His beginning, One is His individuality, His permutation is One"*. This formula emphasises the divine creative force present in all life, and that although we are all separate, yet we are all also interconnected, forming part of the greater whole that is the desire to evolve into perfection.

Kether reminds us of the axiom of *'As above, so below'*, which is phrased in Qabalah as *'Kether is in Malkuth, and Malkuth is in Kether, but after a different fashion.'* It is the absolute divine which we strive towards, but we should not forget that the divine too may reach back towards us. For if we are all interconnected, then our relationship with the external divine should be one of symbiosis, not a parasitic one.

As Kether is the first manifestation from the Limitless Light (*Ain Soph Aur*), the lamp is one of its key symbols, a fact which is worth remembering for ceremonies. The lamp, emanating light, was also one of the main symbols of Theos Hypsistos ('*the Highest God*'), a cult which spread amongst Jews, Christians and Pagans around the Mediterranean around the second century BCE. This cult may well have been another one of the influences on early Qabalah, as suggested by the following second century BCE oracular inscription at Oenoanda in Northern Lycia:

> "*Born of itself, untaught, without a mother, unshakeable, not contained in a name, known by many names, dwelling in fire, this is god. We, his angels, are a small part of god.*"

On the human level, Kether also equates to the *Yechidah* ('*unique essence*' or '*unity*') which is the highest aspect of the *Neshamah* (upper soul). This corresponds to the divine and eternal spark of the soul. It is the most ephemeral and transcendental part of the soul, where the highest essence of man becomes the divine. It is one of the *makifim* ('*envelopments*'), i.e. it is situated around the body, not within it.

Chokmah (ChKMH)

> "*You are wise, shone fixed will from your wisdom, a worker and an artist pulling something from nothing as the light is drawn out from the eye.*"[6]

Sephira	Chokmah (Wisdom)
Number	2
Colour	Grey
Divine Name	IH (Yah)
Archangel	Ratziel
Order of Angels	Ophanim (Wheels), or Kerubim
Heaven	Masloth (Zodiac)
Body	Left side of the Face

---

[6] *Kether Malkuth*, Solomon Gabirol, (1021-1058).

Fragrance	Galbanum, Musk
Virtues	Devotion
Vices	-

Chokmah (pronounced *Hok-mah*, meaning *Wisdom*) is the Sephira of the fixed stars, the outer limits of human perception when viewed in the night sky. It is the place where the divine essence begins to be expressed, as illustrated by *Proverbs 4:7*: *"The beginning is Wisdom: Acquire Wisdom."*

Chokmah is the first emanation from Kether, and begins the process of differentiation, bringing duality onto the Tree of Life. Chokmah is considered the primordial masculine impulse, as Binah is the primordial feminine, both emanating from the androgynous creative energy of Kether. Chokmah represents the left or hidden side of the face, which is still beyond the realm of human perception, though it may be glimpsed in the shadows of space.

Chokmah is the creative impulse of the divine will, and as such mirrors that intent of the will in us as humans. We all have the divine spark within us, which is symbolically represented by the stars in the heavens. The ancients recognised this, and it can be seen in the ancient world, from the Egyptian belief that on death part of the soul became a star in the heavenly body of the stellar goddess Nuit, through to the Greek Orphic Oath of *"I am a child of earth and starry heaven."*

On a physical level our bodies are made of atoms and molecules that were once parts of stars. So the interconnectedness of everything in the universe, all energy, is perfectly expressed in this statement. It encapsulates our aspirations to fulfil our potential and realise the divine spark within us more fully into manifestation. By the light of Chokmah, the pure will permits the template of creation to be unfolded, the perfection and truth of the divine becomes visible to all.

The *Chayah* (or *Chiyah*, meaning *'life force'* or *'living essence'*) is attributed to Chokmah. It is another higher aspect of the part of the soul called the *Neshamah*, which may be viewed as the vitality, or the creative impulse. This may be seen as pure will, the pure will which propels you up the Tree on your quest for perfection.

Binah (BINH)

"For you shall call Understanding [Binah] a Mother."[7]

Sephira	Binah (Understanding)
Number	3
Colour	Black
Divine Name	IHVH (Yahveh)
Archangel	Zaphkiel
Order of Angels	Aralim (Strony and Mighty Ones), or Thrones
Heaven	Shabathai (Saturn)
Body	Right side of face
Fragrance	Civet, Myrrh
Virtues	Silence
Vices	Avarice

Binah (pronounced *Bee-nah*, meaning *Understanding*) is the Sephira of Saturn and of the Great Mother, the Divine Feminine. In the ancient world through until as recently as the eighteenth century, Saturn was perceived as being the outer planet, and as such represented a boundary to man. Beyond Saturn was the vastness of the infinite, which is why Binah is seen as the beginnings of form. Saturn marked the boundary, the moment of transition between force and form. Binah represents the right side of the face, and when gods were portrayed in profile (as on coins), they were usually shown with the right side of the face visible.

There is a saying in modern science that *"evolution occurs at the boundaries"*, and from a mystical perspective we can see a lot of sense in

---

[7] *Proverbs 2:3.*

this. The coastline where the sea and the land meet, or hilltops where air and earth meet are classic examples of places perceived as being imbued with force and good natural spots for performing magick.

However from a more individual perspective, we can say that evolution takes place at the boundaries of our consciousness. We need to discover our boundaries, our limits, before we can transcend them and take another step towards perfection.

Although Binah may be seen as being unattainable as a continuous state of being in human form, being representative of the beginning of a pure energy state, nevertheless we can draw inspiration from the deep panoramic understanding that Binah has to offer. This is why Binah is also known as the 'City of Pyramids'. Although pyramids were places to preserve the dead, they also provide a panoramic view from the top and may have been used for star-gazing, and the top can only be reached by a long ascent from a very large base.

Binah is one of the great keys to the Tree of Life. The more you meditate on the symbolism of Binah, the more you may find yourself able to manipulate your own life and energies in a more positive manner, as you become more aware of the greater web of life around you.

Binah corresponds to the Neshamah, which is the upper soul, breath or pneuma. The Neshamah is also referred to as the Shekinah (which also corresponds to Binah), and is always depicted as being female. The Neshamah is said to reside in the brain (*moach*) of each person. The higher aspects of the Neshamah (the *Chiyah* and *Yechidah*) remain unknown and unknowable to a person until they have become aware of their Neshamah. It is said that all people see the Neshamah at the moment of death, referring to the moment of losing form and becoming soul energy which corresponds to the Binah state as well.

Daath (DAaTh)

"Accept my discipline rather than silver, Knowledge rather than choice gold."[8]

Sephira	Daath (Knowledge)
Number	11
Colour	Lavender
Divine Name	RVACh hQDOSh (Ruach HaQadosh)
Archangel	Anphiel
Order of Angels	-
Heaven	-
Body	Throat
Fragrance	-
Virtues	Confidence, Detachment
Vices	Cowardice, Doubt, Hubris, Isolation

Daath (pronounced Da-art, meaning *Knowledge*) is the interface between the Supernal Triad and the lower Tree. The dew of Kether passes through Daath to fertilise the rest of the Tree, as is recorded in *Proverbs 3:20*, *"By his knowledge the depths are broken up, and the clouds drop down the dew."*

Daath is considered to be the first child of Chokmah and Binah, which did not come to manifestation. It is a paradox, being the *"Sephira that isn't"*. The *Sepher Yetzirah* makes it very clear that Daath is not a Sephira – *"Ten Sephiroth of Nothingness, ten and not nine, ten and not eleven"*. Daath is sometimes considered a Sephira when Kether is seen as being abstract and not a full Sephira.

References to Daath are found throughout important scriptural and mystical texts, such as the *Torah* and *Sepher Raziel Hemelach* (*'The Book of the Angel Raziel'*). Indeed the latter work refers to Daath in the first paragraph of its first book. Daath corresponds to the throat on the human body, the place of speech, where words are created.

---

[8] *Proverbs 8:10.*

As a result Daath can be seen in some respects like a Zen koan, a riddle which confounds the mind – for example, the sound of one hand clapping. Trying to make sense of Daath unless one is experiencing Daath is nonsensical. The only way to really appreciate Daath is from direct experience.

Daath is also intimately connected with the legend of the Fall, for it is the *"Tree of Knowledge (Daath) of Good and Evil"* which Eve and Adam eat the fruit of. Daath then becomes the bridge between the perfection of the Supernal Triad, and the lower Tree, which strives for the lost perfection (of Eden).

In this context we should also note that Daath is used as a symbol for sexual union, with the phrase *"and he knew his wife"*. Thus Daath can also be seen as representing the Hieros Gamos or sacred marriage of Chokmah and Binah, which is why one of its titles is the Bridal Chamber. Likewise references to the concept of a Yesod-Daath Mirror may also be sexual, as the genitals are attributed to Yesod.

Chesed (ChSD)

"The quality of mercy is not strain'd; It droppeth as the gentle rain from heaven; Upon the place beneath."[9]

Sephira	Chesed (Mercy)
Number	4
Colour	Blue
Divine Name	AL (El)
Archangel	Zadkiel
Order of Angels	Chasmalim (Brilliant Ones), or Dominations
Heaven	Tzedeq (Jupiter)
Body	Left hand and arm

---

[9] *The Merchant of Venice*, William Shakespeare (1564-1616).

Fragrance	Cedar, Hyssop
Virtues	Obedience
Vices	Bigotry, Gluttony, Hypocrisy, Tyranny

Chesed (pronounced *Hes-ed,* meaning *Mercy*) is the Sephira of Jupiter. Jupiter is traditionally associated with rulership, and success, hence its alternative name of Gedulah (*'Glory'*). It is the planet associated with religion, but the mysteries contained within a religion rather than the exoteric form or structure. Jupiter embodies the benevolent ruler, dispensing justice with mercy, tempered with authority. Jupiter teaches obedience to the higher cause, when service becomes a pleasure and not just a duty, for the relevance and rightness of the actions can be seen, as well as the benefits of the consequences of such actions.

Chesed is the first reflection of Chokmah, and represents the highest level below the Abyss that form can take before being transmuted to pure force. Chesed is linked with the highest aspects of water, which can be seen as the force that overcomes all. In the *Hekhalot Rabbati* (*'Greater Palaces'*) it is described as *"thousands upon thousands of waves of water ... yet there is not a single drop of water there, only the radiance of the marble stones with which the palace is furnished."* Hence the Pillar of Mercy is also known as the Pillar of Water.

Jupiter is also associated with ascendancy, and gaining a superior position. This includes such areas of life as good bodily health, as well as mental, emotional and spiritual health. Chesed represents the holistic balance of all aspects of the self. Without this balance you cannot cross the Abyss, for it will result in destruction of the self due to lack of integrity.

Chesed is also a place of reconciliation, of ensuring that everything that has been experienced previously is integrated and balanced. This is emphasised by its fourfold nature. Four is a number of balance, and its importance is seen through such expressions as the fourfold name

(Tetragrammaton), and the Four Worlds. Hence Chesed is described in the *Thirty-Two Paths of Wisdom* as *"containing all the holy powers."*

Geburah (GBVRH)

"I arise today; Through a mighty strength,
the invocation of the Trinity;
Through belief in the threeness,
Through confession of the oneness·
Of the Creator of Creation."[10]

Sephira	Geburah (Strength)
Number	5
Colour	Red
Divine Name	ALHIM GBVR (Elohim Givor)
Archangel	Khamael
Order of Angels	Seraphim (Fiery Serpents), or Powers
Heaven	Madim (Mars)
Body	Right hand and arm
Fragrance	Basil, Opoponax
Virtues	Courage, Energy
Vices	Cruelty, Destructiveness

Geburah (pronounced *Ge-voor-ah*, meaning *Strength*) is the Sephira of Mars. It is associated with power and energy. The power of Geburah must be directed by the will, to be power with, or it can turn into the domineering power of control over others, the control of the tyrant or dictator. When it is balanced it represents the force of Justice (*Din*, an alternative name for this Sephira), and when unbalanced it becomes Fear (*Pachad*, another alternative name for Geburah). The only power over we need to be interested in is power over ourselves, the ability to control our actions and keep them in harmony with our wills as manifestations of the divine will. The directed power of Geburah is seen

---

[10] *Lorica*, St Patrick, (387-493).

in the bodily attribution of the right hand and arm, in a world where 90% of the population are right-handed.

Within nature violence is a function of life and the food chain, hence the expression *'nature is red in tooth and claw'*. But this violence is based around killing for food, or to establish hierarchies to breed the healthiest young. It is instinctual violence as part of animal behaviour. Humans have established patterns of behaviour (ethics and laws) to reduce the need for violence. In a social structure violence is usually anti-social, and here we see a different aspect of Geburah, when it is expressed as Justice (*Din*).

The art of the warrior, which can be seen as part of the lessons of Geburah, is about control. Many people do not realise this. A good warrior is assertive rather than aggressive, this is known as *'showing the sword'*. By establishing clear boundaries and showing you will not be dominated, much of the time you can avoid conflict. Sometimes conflict is unavoidable, and then a warrior does the minimum necessary to resolve the situation.

Mars was originally associated with agriculture, and this connection in nature emphasises the benefits of hard work. Having the strength to produce a harvest through directing your energy appropriately is one of the lessons of Mars. So the power of Geburah is the power to do what needs doing, under the direction of the will.

Invisibility is associated with Geburah, and at first it might seem a curious connection. However strength is commonly an invisible quality. The strength of Geburah is not merely physical strength, as exhibited in muscular tone, but spiritual, emotional and mental strength. These are found in people who have persevered and followed their paths. Likewise generally emotional strength is generally more often to be found in women than men, hence the position of Geburah in the Feminine Pillar.

Tiphereth (TPhARTh)

"Beauty enthrones itself, giving itself to the parts as to the sum."[11]

Sephira	Tiphereth (Beauty)
Number	6
Colour	Gold / Yellow
Divine Name	ALVHA (Eloah)
Archangel	Michael
Order of Angels	Malachim (Kings), or Virtues
Heaven	Shamash (Sun)
Body	Heart
Fragrance	Cinnamon, Frankincense, Ginger, Juniper, Rosemary
Virtues	Compassion, Devotion to the Great Work
Vices	Pride

Tiphereth (pronounced *Tif-er-et*, meaning *Beauty*) is the Sephira of the Sun. Tiphereth was also known as *Rachamin*, meaning *Compassion*, which emphasised the spiritual nature of the Tree of Life as a path to personal perfection. As the sun is the centre of our universe, and the heart is the centre of the body, so Tiphereth occupies the centre of the Tree of Life and is attributed to the heart. Long before astronomy accepted a heliocentric view of the universe, the Tree of Life was hinting at this with its central attribution of the sun to Tiphereth.

Tiphereth is the beauty that occupies the pivotal point on the Tree of Life, the text called the *Thirty-Two Paths of Wisdom* says of it:

> *"The Sixth Path is called the Mediating Intelligence, because in it are multiplied the influxes of Emanations; for it causes that influence to flow into all the reservoirs of the blessings with which they themselves are united."*

Tiphereth represents the focused will and intent of the individual, the living fire of divine spirit that burns in the heart and is flamed by the intent of truth and spiritual devotion. This is why it is called the

---

[11] *Enneads I.6.2*, Plotinus (204-270).

'Mediating Intelligence', for it is the point of balance in man, receiving the flow of the universe and directing it in a harmonious manner with his personal genius attached to it.

Tiphereth is also the lower reflection of the unknowable divine of Kether, as the manifest divinity. It represents the divine child, the manifestation of deity. As such it is the point of illumination, the revealing of the mysteries to bring forth Wisdom (Chokmah) and Understanding (Binah). The role of the illuminating energy of Tiphereth is to engender growth and evolution.

Another key to the role of Tiphereth is that it is the point of balance between the directed forces of the upper Tree and their resulting forms in the lower Tree. The higher energies of the Tree find their expression through the centre, and those energies can then manifest into form lower down on the Tree. The heart as the centre of the body corresponds to Tiphereth, and it is interesting to note that the word Tiphereth has the letter Aleph at its heart (in the centre). It is the only Sephira on the Tree which contains the letter Aleph, corresponding to air, and of course the heart is where the oxygen we extract from the air is pumped around the body.

Netzach (NTzCh)

> "Thou who art victory and law
> When empty terrors overawe;
> From vain temptations dost set free,
> And calm'st the weary strife of frail humanity!"[12]

Sephira	Netzach (Victory)
Number	7
Colour	Green
Divine Name	IHVH TzBAVTh (Yahveh Zavaot)

[12] *Ode to Duty*, William Wordsworth (1770-1850).

Archangel	Uriel
Order of Angels	Elohim (Gods), or Principalities
Heaven	Nogah (Venus)
Body	Left hip and leg
Fragrance	Benzoin, Rose, Sandalwood
Virtues	Selflessness
Vices	Hedonism, Lust

Netzach (pronounced Net-zack, meaning *Victory* or *Firmness*) is the Sephira of Venus. Venus is the planet of love, and no other planet (or goddess) has inspired artists, writers and poets as much as she. Love can be experienced in a variety of ways, and this is expressed well through the four Greek words for love – *Agapé* (spiritual love), *Storge* (familial love), *Philia* (brotherly or kinly love), and *Eros* (physical or sexual love), which could be seen as corresponding to the influence of Netzach in the Four Worlds.

The polarity of Netzach and Hod is emphasised in the *Thirty-Two Paths of Wisdom* by the use of the term '*refulgent Splendour*', as splendour is the translation of Hod. Also the intellect is emphasised, and the balance of emotion and intellect is one of the eternal struggles experienced by mankind in seeking to develop and succeed through life.

However as Hod is a lower manifestation on the tree of form from Binah, so is Netzach a lower manifestation on the Tree of the force of Chokmah. For our emotions give force and power to our drives. It is for us to ensure that the emotional charge we create is positive, rather than negative. Negative emotions have a tendency to be stored in our bodies as blockages, and tied up energy that could be used more constructively for our growth.

To master your emotions ensures you can channel their energy into your growth. You can recognise the futility of negative emotions and transform them into their positive counterparts. This includes self-love, though in a positive way where you acknowledge your faults and strive to correct them, not in a narcissistic way.

Throughout the ages the goddesses of love remained unconquered, not for nothing was Aphrodite's Girdle described as being able to bind anything. Love is the strongest force in the universe, and it can help you realise your potential if it is present in your life in a positive way.

Hod (HVD)

"Summer, and noon, and a splendour of silence, felt,
Seen, and heard of the spirit within the sense."[13]

Sephira	Hod (Splendour)
Number	8
Colour	Orange
Divine Name	ALHIM TzBAVTh (Elohim Zavaot)
Archangel	Raphael
Order of Angels	Bene Elohim (Children of the Gods), or Archangels
Heaven	Kohkav (Mercury)
Body	Right hip and leg
Fragrance	Lavender, Lemon, Lime, Storax
Virtues	Humour, Truthfulness
Vices	Dishonesty

Hod (pronounced Hod, and meaning *Splendour*) is the Sephira of Mercury. Mercury is associated with the intellect, and the power of logic and rational thought. In terms of our existence, Hod is our thoughts and ideas. As the fastest moving planet, Mercury is entirely appropriate as the cosmic representative of this power, which on a human level can be seen as the darting quicksilver fire of the nerve synapses firing in our brains, as ideas dart around at the speed of light.

The ability to think logically is often seen as being very cold, and the intellect as being very divorced from feeling and sensing. However this perspective tends to discount the other quality of the intellect,

---

[13] *A Nypholept*, Algernon Swinburne (1837-1909).

which is intuition. This is why the symbol of Mercury is the caduceus, or twin serpent staff. The cold logic of the mind is balanced by the intuitive flashes of inspiration that are also Mercurial in their nature – the black and white serpents of the caduceus. Communication is another Mercurial trait, and a necessary quality, for a good idea means nothing if it is not clearly communicated to others and its benefits spread.

With clear communication should come clear boundaries, another concept associated with Mercury. In ancient Greece piles of stones, called Herms and sacred to Hermes, were placed at boundaries to mark where one realm ended and another began. As the messenger who can travel between the realms, Hermes (and his Roman counterpart Mercury) was the ideal god to also mark those boundaries.

Mythically Mercury is the psychopomp, the guide between the worlds. This role expresses the fluid quality of Mercury, the ability to adapt to ones environment and be at home in any surroundings and circumstances. This is the Splendour of the active mind, able to respond to change and adapt to better ways of functioning. Efficiency could be described as the key word for Hod, the ability not to waste your energy, but rather to use it effectively to always do everything in the best and most appropriate manner.

The other key word for Hod is flexibility. Mercury is nothing if not adaptable, able to undergo immediate changes and be ready to deal with whatever may occur. Flexibility also requires honesty and the ability to exercise clarity and discrimination no matter the circumstances.

Mercury is also associated with healing, of the mind and body. Mercury provides the knowledge and skill needed to practice healing, for the training to be a doctor or healer is a long and arduous process, requiring the mind to be honed like a scalpel to work effectively.

The power of the mind is to give form to ideas, and Hod is a Sephira of form. The experiences of the astral and the imagination of Yesod may be given more form in Hod – through giving a framework to ideas and through being able to manipulate the subtle energies of the astral. The negative side of Mercury is his quicksilver nature which can result in it being difficult to hold onto ideas and inspiration, and here mercury needs to be fixed, made solid by combining it with the manifest power of Malkuth (like cinnabar, mercury sulphide)

Yesod (ISVD)

"Creation's and Creator's crowning good;
Wall of infinitude;
Foundation of the sky,
In Heaven forecast
And long'd for from eternity,"[14]

Sephira	Yesod (Foundation)
Number	9
Colour	Silver
Divine Name	ShDI (Shaddai)
Archangel	Gabriel
Order of Angels	Kerubim (Strong Ones), or Angels
Heaven	Levanah (Moon)
Body	Genitalia
Fragrance	Camphor, Jasmine, Ylang Ylang
Virtues	Independence
Vices	Deception, Idleness

Yesod (pronounced *Yes-od*, and meaning *Foundation*) is the Sephira of the Moon. Traditionally the Moon is associated with the night, and associated nocturnal activities, like dreaming and spells and ceremonies. Hence the name Foundation, for Yesod is the foundation of magical

[14] *To the Body*, Coventry Patmore (1823-1896).

practice, corresponding as it does to both the astral plane and to the unconscious.

Yesod is joined to four other Sephiroth on the Tree, which provides a good analogy to the four phases of the Moon. The 32nd path from Malkuth to Yesod then brings you into Yesod through the New Moon. Opposite this is the 25th path to Tiphereth, which corresponds to the Full Moon. The 30th and 28th paths – to Hod and Netzach respectively, represent the waxing and waning Moon.

The Moon controls the tides on Earth, and Yesod is the higher aspect of Water on the lower Tree, as the next three Sephiroth also embody the higher qualities of the elements in a similar manner. This is why the elemental Archangels are also attributed to planets.

As the realm of the Moon and the astral, Yesod is also associated with ethereal creatures. The four paths connected to Yesod make it the first crossroads we encounter on the Tree. Classically the crossroads is the place of transformation, of death, spirits and ethereal creatures, ruled over by deities such as the Greek Goddess Hekate, with the liminal power they possess.

As Malkuth may be seen as a lower emanation of the energies of Binah, so may Yesod be seen as a lower emanation of Chokmah. Chokmah is creative form, without force, but in Yesod it is in the transitional moment of manifestation from force into form, the creation of manifestation in Malkuth. As a creative essence, Yesod corresponds to the genitals on the human body.

> "The Ninth Path is called the Pure Intelligence because it purifies the Emanations. It proves and corrects the designing of their representations, and disposes the unity with which they are designed without diminution or division."

The preceding description of Yesod from the *Thirty-Two Paths of Wisdom* gives more of an insight into the nature of Yesod. Yesod purifies the emanations, because it is the realm of connection between the conscious mind of man (the microcosm) and the subtle realms that permeate the universe (macrocosm). In the downward flow of energy, Yesod puts the impulses of the higher energies into a form which man can work with. In the upward flow of energy, Yesod is the great barrier, the mirror of truth that causes most to succumb to their own ego and not strive further to the illuminating powers behind it.

Malkuth (MLKVTh)

"Abridgement of delights!
And Queen of sights!
O mine of rarities! O Kingdom wide!
O more! O cause of all! O glorious Bride!"[15]

Sephira	Malkuth (Kingdom)
Number	10
Colour	Brown
Divine Name	ADNI MLK (Adonai Melek)
Archangel	Sandalphon
Order of Angels	Ashim (Flames), or Blessed Souls
Heaven	Cholim Yesodoth (Mundane Foundations)
Body	Feet
Fragrance	Patchouli, Pine, Vetivert
Virtues	Discrimination
Vices	Avarice, Inertia

Malkuth (pronounced *Mal-koot*, meaning *Kingdom*) is the Sephira of the Elements. This refers to the four elements specifically; spirit is not included in this. This is why Malkuth is often depicted as a circle divided into four by an X, separating it into equal quarters for the four elements. This division is also symbolic of the magic circle, with the four cardinal directions indicated by the fourfold division.

---

[15] *Love*, Thomas Traherne (1636-1674).

Malkuth is made up of the principles of the four elements. It is the point of stability and solidity, the objective reality that comprises our existence. As such the process of balance is vital, for when we start on our spiritual journey, we are in the middle of that circle standing at the centre of the crossroads. What path we take is up to us, though the spirit of growth encourages us to have firm roots in the physical but to strive upwards for the light – to become the Tree of Life in miniature, balanced and spreading our branches to realise the potential within.

Malkuth is the only Sephira that is not part of a triad, though it is linked to the three Sephiroth of the Astral Triad (Yesod, Hod and Netzach). Malkuth is said to receive the energies of all the other emanations of the Tree. This is why so many of the titles of Malkuth describe it as a Gate, for it is the Gate to the rest of the Tree of Life, i.e. both the actualisation of the self as the inner Tree, and to other realms as symbolised by the Sephiroth and Worlds. The *Thirty-Two Paths of Wisdom* says of Malkuth:

> *"The Tenth Path is called the Resplendent Intelligence because it is exalted above every head and sits upon the Throne of Binah. It illuminates the splendour of all the Lights, and causes an influence to emanate from the Prince of Countenances, the Angel of Kether."*

The relationships between Malkuth as the physical realm of the elements, with Binah, the beginnings of form, and Kether, the first point of divine manifestation, cannot be overemphasised. When Malkuth is described as *"sitting on the Throne of Binah"*, the relationship is being highlighted. The Throne is a title of Binah, and demonstrates the power of Saturn as the highest aspect of the element of Earth to give solidity and form.

The Shekinah must also be considered within any analysis of Malkuth. Within the Tetragrammaton (IHVH< Yod-Heh-Vav-Heh) we see the feminine influence of the Shekinah (Divine Presence), who is expressed as first as the mother who is the Understanding of Binah (the first Heh) and then through manifestation as the daughter of Malkuth (the final Heh). The energy of Creation that is the initial manifestation of the Greater Shekinah, i.e. the World of Briah containing Binah (Understanding), is manifested in Malkuth through the daughter as the World of Assiah, or Making, also known as the Lesser or Exiled Shekinah. Malkuth represents the making of the creative ideas, the reification of the generative principle in nature, hence nature, the Earth and indeed the Garden of Eden are all referred to as feminine in Qabalah.

There is a Qabalistic saying, *"Kether is in Malkuth, and Malkuth is in Kether, but after a different fashion"*. This is a cumbersome way of expressing the first axiom of hermeticism found on the Emerald Tablet of the alchemists, *"As above, so below"*.

Malkuth is the ultimate reflection of Kether, the manifestation of pure spirit as physical form. Indeed the perception of light as a wave-particle is perfectly described by this relationship. Kether is the light wave, and Malkuth is the manifestation of this energy as the light particle. As the most tangible example of manifestation, Malkuth corresponds to the feet on the human body, which are our point of contact with the earth beneath us.

CHAPTER 3

Connections

There is a saying in modern ecology, which states that *"everything is connected to everything else"*. Nowhere is this more clearly illustrated in spiritual philosophy than in the connections on the Tree of Life. The paths which connect the Sephiroth of the Tree are fundamental to its nature, creating patterns like the Pillars and Triads through which different aspects of the Qabalah, and by extension the self, are expressed. The dynamic relationships between different parts of the Tree are an essential part of the vitality of Qabalah, giving life to the philosophies and practices.

The Evolution of the Tree of Life

The pattern of the paths has varied over the centuries, which can be confusing if you are presented with different variants of the Tree with no explanation. The first known depiction of the Tree of Life comes from 1516, on the cover of the book *Portae Lucis* (*'Gates of Light'*) by Paul Riccius, a Jew who converted to Christianity. The book was a Latin translation of the Hebrew work *Shaare Orah* (which also means *Gates of Light*) by Rabbi Joseph Gkatalia (1248-1323 CE). The cover is a famous image, showing an old man holding a Tree of Life.

The image is different in a number of significant ways to all the subsequent images, not least by the fact that there are only sixteen paths. Some of the most significant paths are absent, such as two of the cross-paths and Kether-Tiphereth. One particularly important aspect of the image is that the old man holds the Tree of Life as you would a tool, emphasising its practical nature.

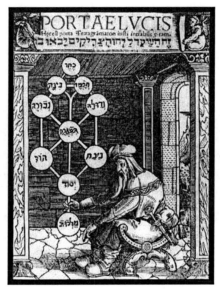

THE COVER IMAGE OF PORTAE LUCIS

The next model is the Lurianic Tree of Life, created by the Ari. Rabbi Isaac Luria, often known as the Ari (1534-72 CE) is arguably the greatest Qabalist who ever lived, and the version of the Tree of Life usually associated with Jewish Kabbalah is commonly called the Lurianic Tree of Life after him. In this model, the paths from Netzach and Hod to Malkuth are absent, leaving Malkuth only connected to Yesod. The additional two paths to replace (precede) these are from Chokmah to Geburah and from Binah to Chesed.

A detour on the development of the Tree of Life was provided by the English Rosicrucian mystic, astrologer and Paracelsian physicist Robert Fludd (1574-1637 CE). Amongst his many works is a stylised image of the Tree of Life, with the pillars reversed and most of the paths missing, though interestingly he did particularly emphasise the Orders of Angels.

The model now used as the standard image in Qabalah in the Western Mystery Tradition is the Kircher Tree of Life. Athanasius Kircher was a German Jesuit scholar (1602-80 CE). In 1651-3 he published the three volume *Oedipus Aegyptiacus*, a study of Egyptology which drew on various sources, and included his image of the Tree of Life.

With Kircher comes one of the most dramatic changes to the geography of the Tree of Life, which is the change of attributions of the Hebrew letters. Prior to Kircher the Hebrew Kabbalah worked with the very logical system of the three Mother letters to the cross-paths, the seven Double letters to the vertical paths and the twelve Single letters to the diagonal paths. Kircher changed this so the attributions were based on the Sephiroth. Thus the order was sequential from the top of the Tree to the bottom, working through the Hebrew alphabet, giving a completely different set of attributions.

A final Tree of Life we should mention is that of the Gra. Rabbi Elijah ben Solomon, best known as the Gra (1720-97 CE), created an entirely symmetrical, and more radically different Tree of Life. Tiphereth is moved up to the Abyss where Daath normally resides (or not). Yesod is then moved up to the place of Tiphereth. This means Tiphereth is no longer joined to Netzach and Hod, and Yesod becomes connected to Chesed and Geburah.

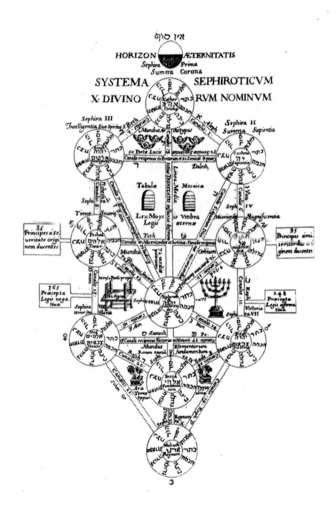

THE TREE OF LIFE, ATHANASIUS KIRCHER (PUBLISHED 1653)

The Path Attributions of the Hebrew Letters

The following table shows how the attributions of the Hebrew letters, and indeed the positions of paths have changed:

Path Connecting	Ari Model	Gra Model	Kircher Model (common use)
1-2	Heh	Heh	Aleph
1-3	Vav	Vav	Beth
1-6	Daleth	Beth	Gimel
2-3	Shin	Shin	Daleth
2-4	Beth	Gimel	Vav
2-5	Zain	-	-
2-6	Teth	Ain	Heh
3-4	Qoph	-	-
3-5	Gimel	Daleth	Cheth
3-6	Ayin	Cheth	Zain
4-5	Aleph	Aleph	Teth
4-6	Cheth	Teth	Yod
4-7	Kaph	Kaph	Kaph
4-9	-	Lamed	-
5-6	Tzaddi	Yod	Lamed
5-8	Peh	Peh	Mem
5-9	-	Nun	-
6-7	Yod	-	Nun
6-8	Samekh	-	Ayin
6-9	Resh	Resh	Samekh
7-8	Mem	Mem	Peh
7-9	Nun	Samekh	Tzaddi
7-10	-	Taddi	Qoph
8-9	Lamed	Ayin	Resh
8-10	-	Qoph	Shin
9-10	Tav	Tav	Tav

The Three Pillars

> *"When the Holy One, blessed be He, sits on the throne of judgement, Justice stands on his right hand, Mercy on his left, and Truth stands directly facing Him."*[16]

The Sephiroth of the Tree of Life all lie vertically within three columns, known as Pillars. These three pillars represent many concepts and symbols, most of which revolve around the idea of a central balancing harmony between two opposing forces. The three pillars are also referred to as the *zahzahoth* (*'hidden splendours'*), a term which implies the underlying balance of the opposing forces of primordial mercy and primordial justice by primordial will.

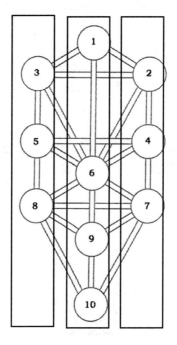

---

[16] *3 Enoch 48.*

An early Biblical reference to the Black and White Pillars occurs in *I Kings 7:14*, where the artisan Hiram (the first Freemason) who worked on the Temple is described as *"Filled with wisdom and understanding and skill"*. As the Temple itself corresponds to the Tree of Life, it can be seen that Hiram is being likewise compared with the pillars, by being filled with wisdom (Chokmah) and understanding (Binah), the capitals of the two outer Pillars. Likewise the middle Pillar is being implied by the word *'skill'*.

Severity	Harmony	Mercy
Black	Grey	White
Right side of body	Spine/Centre line	Left side of body
Form	Transition	Force
Matter	Spirit	Energy
Negative	Neutral	Positive
Passive	Stillness	Active
Feminine	Androgyne	Masculine
Fire	Air	Water
Restraint/Constriction	Equilibrium	Expansion
Binah, Geburah, Hod	Kether, (Daath), Tiphereth, Yesod, Malkuth	Chokmah, Chesed, Netzach

The Three Triads

The Sephiroth of the Tree of Life divide into three triads, with Malkuth being the only Sephira not included in a triad. These triads form as a repeating pattern that occurs down the Tree, of force and form balancing into action or intent. A good description of this was given by the Renaissance humanist and church scholar John Colet, when he observed of the orders of angels (in their triads of the three hierarchies, superior, middle and inferior):

> "Thus does God beam forth with firmness, wisdom, and love in the Thrones, Kerubs, and Seraphs, which threefold system of the Divine Ray goes forth, and causes that in the Powers, Virtues, and Dominions there should be reflected His divine and firm Power, His wise Virtue, and the most loving Dominion."[17]

The Supernal Triad

The first triad on the Tree is of the first three Sephiroth of Kether, Chokmah and Binah, which together make the Archetypal World of Atziluth. It is the only triad that forms a triangle with its apex upwards, indicating the divine nature of the forces contained in this triad. It also shows the initial separation of the divine essence into separate components. The Sephiroth of the Supernal Triad are sometimes referred to as the Superior Crowns, as each of the Sephiroth crowns a pillar on the Tree.

This triad is referred to in *Job 28:11-12*, "He bindeth the floods from overflowing; and the thing that is hid bringeth he forth to light (i.e. Kether). But where shall wisdom (Chokmah) be found? And where is the place of understanding (Binah)?"

---

17 *Works*, Colet, C16.

The Supernal Triad also corresponds to the upper soul, or *Neshamah*. The *Neshamah* has two higher aspects, the *Chiyah* and the *Yechidah*. Thus each of the three Sephiroth have a part of the higher soul attributed to them, Kether with the *Yechidah*, Chokmah with the *Chiyah* and Binah with the *Neshamah*.

The Ethical Triad

The second triad on the Tree is made by the fourth, fifth and sixth Sephiroth of Chesed, Geburah and Tiphereth. It is also known as *'the Children'*, referring to the position below the Father (Chokmah) and Mother (Binah) in the Supernal Triad. The names of Ethical and Moral for this triad emphasise an important quality associated with this area of the Tree of Life. The focus of the energy moves from being inwards to outwards. The inner mastery gained in the Astral Triad below is balanced in the apex of this triad at Tiphereth, and then radiated outwards to the world. If you are in a state of balance and harmony, this is expressed in an ethical and moral manner, with strength (Geburah) and mercy (Chesed) colouring your actions.

That this triad is associated with action may also be seen by its correspondence to the body. Tiphereth corresponds to the heart, and is the centre of balance. Chesed and Geburah correspond to the left and right arms and hands, the doing part of the body. With our hands we act, through writing, manipulation of tools, etc. So this triad is very much associated with the outer action of the will, manifesting your intent.

The Astral Triad

The third triad, also known as the Vegetative Triad, comprises the seventh, eighth and ninth Sephiroth of Netzach, Hod and Yesod. It is also known as *'the Grandchildren'*, referring to its position as the third triad, under the *'Children'* of the Ethical Triad.

These three Sephiroth are the ones which concentrate on your inner state. They are associated with the emotions (Netzach), mind (Hod) and unconscious (Yesod). The balance of these inner states to reach a point where you are acting in harmony with yourself, rather than hindering your own progress, is one of the first major steps that need to be taken on the journey up the Tree of Life. Through mastering the unconscious, the intellect and the emotions the seeker may then burst through the rainbow of Paroketh to the realisation of pure will that is Tiphereth.

When the Ethical Triad and the Astral Triad are combined together they are also known as the *'Sephiroth of Construction'* (*Sephiroth ha-Benyin*), being the forces which are closest to and act upon the physical plane. They are also the six Sephiroth which correspond to the six days of creation in Genesis as the days of the week (excluding the Sabbath).

Triad	Supernal	Ethical	Astral
Contains	Kether, Chokmah, Binah	Chesed, Geburah, Tiphereth	Netzach, Hod, Yesod
World	Atziluth	Briah	Yetzirah
Also called	Intellectual World	Moral World The Children	Natural World The Grandchildren
Soul	Neshamah (Higher Soul)	Ruach (Breath)	Nephesh (Animal Soul)
Body	Head	Torso and arms	Legs, genitalia and feet

The Knowledge Triad

A triad may also be made downwards from Chokmah and Binah, with its apex in Daath. This triad is also known as the Triad of Truth, for Truth is said to be made of Wisdom, Understanding and Knowledge. From this triad comes the saying *"Knowledge is the child of Wisdom and Understanding"*.

The Knowledge Triad is especially referred to in the book of *Proverbs*. Hence we see it in *Proverbs 2:6*, *"For the Lord giveth wisdom [Chokmah]: out of his mouth cometh knowledge [Daath] and understanding [Binah]."*

It is found again in *Proverbs 3:19-20* in connection with the dew which represents the divine light, *"The Lord by wisdom [Chokmah] hath founded the earth: by understanding [Binah] hath he established the heavens. By his knowledge [Daath] the depths are broken up, and the clouds drop down the dew."*

Dew was a term often used to denote the gaining of heavenly knowledge (of Kether), for it is found in the morning as the sun rises, having descended from the heavens to settle on the grass (earth).

CHAPTER 4

The Paths

"With thirty-two mystical paths of Wisdom engraved Yah"[18]

The thirty-two mystical paths of the Tree of Life are expressed through the ten numbers (one to ten) and the twenty-two Hebrew letters. Combined they give the ten Sephiroth (also called numerations) and twenty-two connecting paths. Significantly, thirty-two is also the numerical value of the Hebrew word *lev* (LB), meaning *'heart'*, which indicates that the Tree of Life is the heart of the Qabalah.

In Hebrew, the word used for the paths is *Netivot* (NThIBVTh). This is not the common word for path, *Derekh* (DRK), which indicates a public path. A *Nativ* (NThIB) is a personal path, one which is hidden, with no signposts, and refers to the path of the individual, which they must make for themselves. Another word for path is *Orach* (ARCh), which is related to the *Ruach* (RVCh). Ruach means *spirit* or *wind*, and can also mean *direction*, and so implies both motion and the indwelling divine spirit. This term is hence particularly appropriate for the paths, though it is not the one generally used.

The word Nativ adds to 462, which is twice 231, the number of Gates created by combining each letter with the other letters of the Hebrew alphabet. Each permutation contains 2 letters, giving 462 letters in total. Thus the paths offer the way up and down the Tree (2 x 231).

---

[18] *Sepher Yetzirah 1:1.*

This is particularly significant in light of the techniques using the 231 Gates.

The paths are also described as *'paths of wisdom'*, indicating Chokmah, implying the flow from the highest point of Kether (1) to Chokmah (2) and so to the rest of the Tree of Life. The Tree of Life is also known as *Chokmah Nistorah*, the *'secret or hidden wisdom'*. This is referred to in *Sepher Rezial Hemelach*, where it says, *"The secret of two is thirty-two most glorious trodden paths, hidden by wisdom."*[19]

The attributions used for the paths must be considered before launching further into their symbolism. The Jewish Kabbalistic Tree of Life has a simple system of attributions, i.e. the Mother Letters on the horizontal paths, the Double Letters on the vertical paths and the Single Letters on the diagonal paths. However these attributions are to the earlier model of the Tree of Life, as given by the Ari (see the earlier section, *The Evolution of the Tree of Life*), which has differences to the one used in the Western Mystery Tradition.

The attributions used today in the Western Mystery Tradition were not created by the Hermetic Order of the Golden Dawn as popularly perceived. Kircher's image of the Tree of Life in *Oedipus Aegypticus*, published in 1653, two hundred and thirty-five years earlier, was already using the attributions of the Hebrew letters to the paths on the image of the Tree of Life which has become the accepted standard.

Although it does not have the same simplicity through appropriate division of letter types to path types used in Jewish Kabbalah, the Western mystery Tradition system does have its own coherence of attribution. Thus the first three paths and letters come off Kether, the next three off Chokmah, the next two off Binah, etc.

---

[19] *The Holy Names, Sepher Rezial Hemelach.*

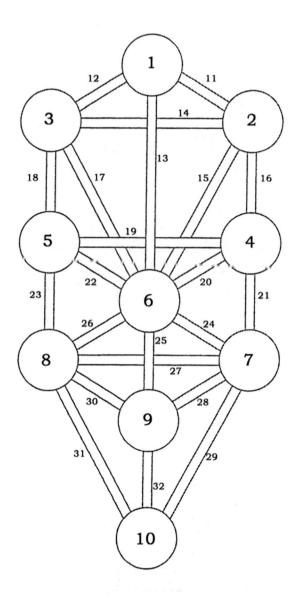

THE PATHS AND THEIR NUMBERS

Working with the Paths

To explore the Paths of the Tree of Life in depth would require a separate work, but it is important that we explore the most important considerations for practical work. Where the Sephiroth correspond to the major parts of the body, the Paths can be seen as symbolically corresponding to the arteries and veins, the muscles and ligaments, which connect them. A result of this is the beneficial use of the Paths for energy work such as healing on the self, ensuring you remain in a balanced and harmonious state.

The Paths balance and harmonise the forces of the Sephiroth, providing the connections which give the Tree of Life form. As such they represent energies of equilibrium and transformation. Pathworking (guided visualisation meditation) has become a popular method of working with the Paths, but there are many other techniques that can also be used to benefit from the energies of the Paths. It is important that you immerse yourself in the symbols and patterns of a Path every bit as fully as you would when working with a Sephira.

We have included appropriate Psalms for working with the paths for different results. The Psalms have a long and practical history of magical use, particularly in connection with the grimoires and Qabalah, with their emphasis on Qabalistic symbolism. We have drawn particularly on works such as *Sepher Shimmush Tehillim* ('The Book of the Use of the Psalms') and *Livre d'Or* ('The Book of Gold'), both of which are eighteenth century texts. The Psalms may be spoken in English, or if you prefer, Latin, or Hebrew.

The technique of Unification of the Divine Names may also be used with the paths to great effect. This provides a different type of focus to using the Divine Names provided for the Paths, drawing as it does on the Sephiroth on both ends of the path.

The Divine Names we have provided for the paths are based on our own work. These were drawn from the path attributions of the archangels and heavens, as these give a starting point to ensure an appropriate creative energy is being applied. Additionally we determined the attributions of the Orders of Angels through the archangels and heavens in a similar way, to ensure that the hierarchy of angels is fully represented throughout the Tree.

32nd Path – The Path of Dreams

Position	Malkuth – Yesod
Letter	Tav
Magick	Magical Oath, developing Discrimination, giving Form
Divine Name	Jahveh
Archangel	Zaphkiel
Angels	Aralim
Attribution	Saturn
Colour	Indigo
Fragrance	Myrrh
Mineral	Smoky Quartz
Psalms	137

This is the first path you walk on the Tree, and it connects the material plane (Malkuth, the elements) to the realms of dreams and the astral (Yesod), the unconscious connection to the subtle web of forces that connects us.

As the first path, it marks the decision to follow a spiritual path, and the changes this may bring. For this reason it has often been likened to an underworld journey, a symbolic death of the material self. This also equates to the practice of discrimination, and starting to dispel the baggage you have been carrying that holds you back and drains your energy.

Saturn can be both the giver of form and the devourer, and these can both be reflected in the changes which occur to the mundane and spiritual lives. This path is exemplified by the magical oath, which marks the commitment or covenant between yourself and the divine to fulfil your potential and realise your genius.

31st Path – The Path of Clarity

Position	Malkuth – Hod
Letter	Shin
Magick	Improving Memory, developing Clarity, Study
Divine Name	Eloah
Archangel	Michael
Angels	Malachim
Attribution	Fire
Colour	Glowing Red
Fragrance	Saunderswood
Mineral	Cat's Eye
Psalms	65, 134

This path is that of mental focus, the fire in the mind that gives clarity, hence its role connecting Malkuth to Hod. It is the calm force of reason that enables us to make clear decisions after having weighed up all the options.

This path is one of the root paths from Malkuth, connecting the external physical world with the internal mental world. As such it is a path of harmonisation, of balancing the mental and physical. This is often achieved through study to develop either or both the mental world and physical skills.

As time passes, so the memory becomes ever more useful to the seeker, and this is reflected in the burning fire of Shin with its three tongues, representing knowledge (past), experience (present) and precognition or intuition (future).

30th Path – The Path of Intuition

Position	Yesod – Hod
Letter	Resh
Magick	Developing Intuition, exploring Symbols & Dreams (including Divination), gaining Information
Divine Name	Eloah
Archangel	Michael
Angels	Malachim
Attribution	Sun
Colour	Yellow
Fragrance	Ginger
Mineral	Amber
Psalms	23

This path connects the rational and logical parts of the conscious mind with the unconscious mind, and the exchange of information and ideas which flow both ways. It also helps you focus on the subtle influences in divinations.

Because you are working more with subtle ideas on this path, including dreams and intuition and the psychic senses (for divination), this path is one which can cause your perception of reality to start to go a little fuzzy around the edges. In such circumstances work in Malkuth and on the 32nd or 31st path will help things become more grounded and focused again.

This path can also bring an increased awareness of the presence of non-physical spiritual creatures. These should not be allowed to distract you, which they may seek to do. Remember that any interaction with spiritual creatures should be both beneficial and symbiotic. They are often very good at glamour and do not have a human moral code, so caution is always recommended.

29th Path – The Path of Glamour

Position	Malkuth – Netzach
Letter	Qoph
Magick	Creating Glamour, developing the Magical Personality, releasing baggage or trauma
Divine Name	Elon
Archangel	Barchiel
Angels	Kerubim
Attribution	Pisces
Colour	Violet-Red
Fragrance	Ylang Ylang
Mineral	Amethyst
Psalms	40, 51

This path links the emotional self to the material world and mundane existence. As such it is connected to the image we choose to portray ourselves with, the masks we wear in different surroundings.

This path is also associated with the lower levels of the astral, where glamour and illusion are rife. Discrimination is critical on this path, as illusion can all too easily lead to delusion if not countered with common sense and discernment.

As this path encourages the release of emotional baggage and resolution of traumas, both of which may have been blocking and storing a lot of personal power, there can be a tendency to disperse the energy when it is released, instead of focusing it into growth and strengthening intent. For this reason it can be beneficial to maintain austerity whilst working this path.

28th Path – The Path of Passion

Position	Yesod – Netzach
Letter	Tzaddi
Magick	Focusing Emotional Intent, working with Sexuality, Sigil work
Divine Name	Yahveh
Archangel	Cambiel

Angels	Aralim
Attribution	Aquarius
Colour	Violet
Fragrance	Copal
Mineral	Kyanite
Psalms	45, 46

This path is like a powerful undercurrent in a river, the connection between emotions and the unconscious. As such it is a path which requires great focus, but offers great rewards, e.g. for planting sigils in the unconscious.

As the path which unites the powers of the Moon and Venus, this is another cautionary path. The unconscious can overflow into your mundane life with this path, and emotions run strong like rivers, so you need to remain focused.

Passion can lead to obsession, a common problem in ritual work, which is why e.g. sigils are so often destroyed after creation or a period of use. The emotional power must be balanced by the intellectual power, to maintain balance, which is the central theme to successfully ascending the Tree.

27th Path – The Path of Harmony

Position	Hod – Netzach
Letter	Peh
Magick	Developing Communication Skills, developing Decisiveness, Lucid Dreaming
Divine Name	Agla
Archangel	Khamael
Angels	Seraphim
Attribution	Mars
Colour	Scarlet-Red
Fragrance	Dragon's Blood
Mineral	Garnet
Psalms	31, 42

This path unites the twin poles of intellect and emotion, thereby providing a wealth of power if the balance is right. Like a scales the harmony must be maintained, and if it is the result is greater control over subtle work.

As the first cross-path encountered on the Tree, it is a checkpoint to ensure you are in equilibrium before continuing on your journey. It is the last path before passing through the veil of Paroketh towards Tiphereth. If you have worked the paths successfully the veil will be like a gossamer thin rainbow. The more resistance you encounter above the 27th path, the less you have completed below it.

The letter Peh means 'mouth', and this path is connected with words, both in developing communication, and also in being accomplished at vibrating words of power to enhance your practices.

26th Path – The Path of Healing

Position	Hod – Tiphereth
Letter	Ayin
Magick	Healing, dealing with Egotism, achieving Promotion or Advancement
Divine Name	Yahveh
Archangel	Hanael
Angels	Ashim
Attribution	Capricorn
Colour	Blue-Violet
Fragrance	Vetivert
Mineral	Onyx
Psalms	14, 47

This path connects the two healing planets, acting as a channel for curing magick. The heart connection (Tiphereth) emphasises the need for balance and reminds us that such healing is done by drawing energy in, not using our own.

This path penetrates through the Veil of Paroketh, forming part of the journey to self-realisation, which means the ego should be controlled by this point, or the veil will thicken and impede your progression.

The letter Ayin means *'eye'*, and this is significant in emphasising both our normal eyes and the third eye. Both are necessary when dealing with the manipulation of delicate energies, which healing is. Clear vision is also essential for further progression, to avoid being misled.

25th Path – The Path of Lesser Reflection

Position	Yesod – Tiphereth
Letter	Samekh
Magick	Boosting power levels, creating Harmony, Self-empowerment
Divine Name	Elon
Archangel	Adnachiel
Angels	Kerubim
Attribution	Sagittarius
Colour	Blue
Fragrance	Saffron
Mineral	Turquoise
Psalms	115, 118

This path is extremely significant, uniting as it does the Sun (Tiphereth) and Moon (Yesod). It connects the intent and will with the unconscious or subtle realms, making it the idea path for strengthening the self or empowering rites.

As the sun's light is reflected by the moon, so this path can reflect the energy of the upper Tree. This means the divine power of the supernal triad starts to become accessible at this point, and should be harnessed to boost development up the Tree.

As part of the Middle Pillar, , and being attributed to the letter Samekh (meaning *'prop'*) this path can be seen as part of your magical spine, and it is essential that you strengthen this path of polarity between will and unconscious.

24th Path – The Path of Love

Position	Netzach – Tiphereth
Letter	Nun
Magick	Expanding on existing Frameworks/Energies, developing Élan/Grace, dispelling negative Self-Image
Divine Name	Agla
Archangel	Barbiel
Angels	Bene Elohim
Attribution	Scorpio
Colour	Green-Blue
Fragrance	Benzoin
Mineral	Serpentine
Psalms	15, 57, 75

This path unites the principles of love (Netzach) and Will (Tiphereth), giving intent to passion, and thus being a path of expansion and realisation. This path encourages the development of grace and élan in the magician.

As with the other Paroketh paths (26th and 25th), this can be a challenging path to work with. At this point you should cultivate (if you have not already done so) self-love and should have a strong sense of self-esteem (without hubris).

When you work on this path you may find you radiate a stronger than usual charisma into the world, resulting in people being more attracted to you. This is something to be aware of, and not abuse or allow to flatter your ego.

23rd Path – The Path of Dissolution

Position	Hod – Geburah
Letter	Mem
Magick	Dispelling old Ideas, overcoming Obstacles, propagating Knowledge
Divine Name	El Chi
Archangel	Gabriel
Angels	Kerubim
Attribution	Water
Colour	Deep Blue
Fragrance	Dammar
Mineral	Aquamarine
Psalms	28, 131

This path is one of action and moving forward, connecting the dynamism of Mars (Geburah) with the swiftness of Mercury (Hod) through the transformative power of the element of water. It is also good for dispelling outdated ideas and concepts.

As another Paroketh path, it is one which will help strip away anything outmoded that you have not let go of yet. Dissolution is a necessary part of the process – the 'solve' of 'solve et coagula'.

As a knowledge path, this path is a good one to work with when you need to spread ideas or information to others, whether it be by spoken word, written or electronic form.

22nd Path – The Path of Action

Position	Tiphereth – Geburah
Letter	Lamed
Magick	Completing Projects, strengthening Will, winning Competitions
Divine Name	Owlam
Archangel	Zuriel
Angels	Elohim
Attribution	Libra
Colour	Green

Fragrance	Geranium
Mineral	Peridot
Psalms	20, 72

This path is one of dynamism, which connects the two fiery Sephiroth of the Tree, Geburah (Mars) to Tiphereth (Sun). The concentration of these forces makes this path a path of completion and achievement.

It could be described as a *'straight and narrow'* path, as the *'ox-goad'* (Lamed) of your intent helps remain focused on your goals so that you achieve completion, seeing projects to fruition or winning through in difficult situations.

This is also a path of consequences, as any successful result will always have results, which ripple out and affect others. How your actions affect other people becomes something to consider more as you move higher up the Tree.

21st Path – The Path of Fortune

Position	Tiphereth – Chesed
Letter	Kaph
Magick	Developing your Fortune or Business, improving Luck, winning Games
Divine Name	Elon
Archangel	Zadkiel
Angels	Chasmalim
Attribution	Jupiter
Colour	Royal Blue
Fragrance	Sage
Mineral	Turquoise
Psalms	4, 5, 82

This path is one of the most important because it represents the random element of luck. There can always be a random event, and so it is good to harness such windows of opportunity. Additionally of course it applies to improving your fortunes.

These two planets (Sun and Jupiter) were known as the Benefics in medieval times, which emphasises the positive nature of this path. This path is really one for taking the world in the *'palm of your hand'* (Kaph).

This path is best approached when things are in balance, so the benefits are maximised. If you work this path when things are problematic, it is likely to act as a balance and return things to a neutral state, rather than making them hugely positive.

20th Path – The Path of Devotion

Position	Tiphereth – Chesed
Letter	Yod
Magick	Devotional Work, Emotional Growth, Fertility
Divine Name	Elohim
Archangel	Hamaliel
Angels	Malachim
Attribution	Virgo
Colour	Yellow-Green
Fragrance	Pine
Mineral	Agate
Psalms	11, 12, 129

This path unites intent (Tiphereth) with benevolence (Chesed), providing the basis for devotional work. It enables the development of positive emotional states, and fertility of ideas and feelings.

This path is one for actively pursuing your link with divinity, which can help you expand your perceptions of deity within and without. It is also beneficial for emotional development, and dealing with any remaining emotional baggage which has not yet been resolved.

If you need to increase the fertility of something, be it yourself, a project, a field, or whatever it may be, then this path is also a very good one to work with.

19th Path – The Path of Strength

Position	Geburah – Chesed
Letter	Teth
Magick	Directing Events, cultivating Benevolence, achieving Balance
Divine Name	Eloah
Archangel	Verchiel
Angels	Seraphim
Attribution	Leo
Colour	Yellow
Fragrance	Cinnamon
Mineral	Tiger's Eye
Psalms	8, 16

This path unites the twin poles of Mercy (Chesed) and Strength (Geburah), or Glory (Gedulah) and Fear (Pachad). It is a path of equilibrium, of being at the eye of the storm, where you can direct events to achieve your goals.

When you apply strength, you need to do so with a careful touch, to ensure the strength is properly used and no damage is caused. Hence this is a path of balance, as the second of the cross paths on the Tree of Life.

As the path of the serpent (Teth), this is another path where personal magetism may be increased through work, resulting in an increase in sexual interest. If so remember the principles of balance.

18th Path – The Path of Influence

Position	Geburah – Binah
Letter	Cheth
Magick	Creating Major Change, extending your Influence, dispersing Malefic Energy
Divine Name	El Chi
Archangel	Muriel
Angels	Chasmalim
Attribution	Cancer
Colour	Orange-Yellow

Fragrance	Ylang Ylang
Mineral	Pearl
Psalms	7, 9, 10, 92

This path crosses from the action of Geburah to the liminal state of Binah, where force and form meet. This path is one for effecting major change, particularly when it is life-changing events, e.g. career change, moving country.

This path is the first of the Abyss paths, which by its nature implies change, as the emphasis is moving into the connection with the subtle (and not so subtle) divine forces.

It is also good for banishing negative influences, whether it be those resulting from situations, places or other people. The ability to extend your sphere of influence is also emphasised on this path.

17th Path – The Path of Personal Power

Position	Tiphereth – Binah
Letter	Zain
Magick	Accepting your Destiny, developing Psychic Abilities, connecting to the Shekinah
Divine Name	Elohim
Archangel	Ambriel
Angels	Aralim
Attribution	Gemini
Colour	Orange
Fragrance	Lavender
Mineral	Alexandrite
Psalms	104

This path combines the intent and will of the magician (Tiphereth) with the psychic senses and instincts (Binah). It thus represents the personal power of the seeker, by being the connection of the Neshamah and Ruach.

This could also be called the path of kingship (or queenship) as it is the point where the middle soul (Ruach) and upper soul (Neshamah) meet, and as such is a path of revelation and transformation.

The results of such a union include an increase in personal abilities and an acceptance of your path. It could be likened to a moment of realisation where many things suddenly become clear and the shadows fade away leaving an illuminated path ahead.

16th Path – The Path of Ascendancy

Position	Chesed – Chokmah
Letter	Vav
Magick	Assuming Superiority, increasing Creative Power, Astrology
Divine Name	Owlam
Archangel	Asmodel
Angels	Ophanim
Attribution	Taurus
Colour	Red-Orange
Fragrance	Patchouli
Mineral	Jade
Psalms	34

This path is one of assuming a superior position, connecting the established material power of Jupiter (Chesed) with the supernal stellar power (Chokmah). This connection is one of creative power and its expression.

The power of this path is externalised as directed force to achieve specific goals. By this point you may well have become somewhat detached from mundane society, and it is important that you do not let hubris take you and undo all of your hard work.

It should be remembered that Chesed is also called Gedulah (glory), and pride in your work is acceptable, but as in all things balance must be maintained to ensure you do not hinder yourself.

15th Path – The Path of Destiny

Position	Tiphereth – Chokmah
Letter	Heh
Magick	Enhancing Willpower, realising Full Potential, spreading a Magical Current
Divine Name	Agla
Archangel	Malchidael
Angels	Chaioth HaQadosh
Attribution	Aries
Colour	Red
Fragrance	Basil
Mineral	Bloodstone
Psalms	108

This path is the stellar path, connecting the sun (Tiphereth) to the stars (Chokmah). It is a path for realising your potential and manifesting it into the world, shining as brightly as you can and radiating truth and positive evolution.

At this point you should be spreading the magical current you work, which means your activities will be largely focused around helping others enhance their lives, through whatever assistance may be required, e.g. healing, blessings, dispersing negativity, etc.

Destiny can also indicate acceptance, and service to the creative divine essence. Here the seeker must come to terms with the difference between acceptance and submission, which is all based on attitude.

14th Path – The Path of Union

Position	Binah – Chokmah
Letter	Daleth
Magick	Enhancing Opposite Gender Connection, Personal Reification, removing Inappropriate People
Divine Name	Owlam
Archangel	Uriel
Angels	Elohim
Attribution	Venus
Colour	Emerald Green

Fragrance	Rose
Mineral	Malachite
Psalms	27, 97

This path represents the ultimate connection of feminine and masculine, and as such is a path of personal reification. It is also a path for enhancing your connection with the opposite gender, particularly those close to you, though it also engages discrimination, so you may choose to cut some people loose if they are parasitic.

By exploring the inner divine, the doorway (Daleth) to the *makifim* (*'envelopments'*) is opened. This is the beginning of the process of realising and uniting the external aspects of the soul with the internal, emphasised by this being the final cross path moving up the Tree.

This path may produce feelings from deep in the unconscious, from your distant past, which cause you to feel you have taken several steps backward. From this perspective it can be quite a humbling path.

13th Path – The Path of Greater Reflection

Position	Tiphereth – Kether
Letter	Gimel
Magick	Connecting Divine Within & Without, Removing the Last Illusions, Vision of the Divine
Divine Name	El Chi
Archangel	Gabriel
Angels	Kerubim
Attribution	Moon
Colour	Violet
Fragrance	Camphor
Mineral	Moonstone
Psalms	

This path is the one through Daath, and could be seen as the path of smoke and mirrors. It is ultimately a path of connection to the divine, from within to without, but this requires passing the tests of Daath, which can bounce you back to Yesod if you are not ready.

As with the 14th path, this is a challenging path which gives you a reality check, and reminds you the road is long, even when you think you are near the end!

This path leads through Daath, the Sephira that is not. As such it is a path which should be explored in silence, and the dispersal of chattering voices, both within and without, should be ignored.

12th Path – The Path of Attainment

Position	Binah – Kether
Letter	Beth
Magick	Knowledge of the Inner Divine, spreading your Intent, manifesting a Magical Current
Divine Name	Elohim
Archangel	Raphael
Angels	Bene Elohim
Attribution	Mercury
Colour	Orange
Fragrance	Storax
Mineral	Opal
Psalms	99

This path demonstrates the attainment of knowledge of the inner divine, and the ability to begin expressing it. It is a path of pure intent, the spreading of blessings, the divine light shining forth.

This path is involved with the manifesting of truth, not simply spreading it. At this point you will be entirely on the path of intent, and should be compassionately efficient in your behaviour.

The benevolence of divine inspiration is tempered with active force on this path, which encourages action, it is not a passive path!

11th Path – The Path of Perfection

Position	Chokmah – Kether
Letter	Aleph
Magick	Ensuring Perfection, knowing the Divine, realising Genius
Divine Name	Elohim
Archangel	Raphael
Angels	Bene Elohim
Attribution	Air
Colour	Bright Yellow
Fragrance	Elemi
Mineral	Topaz
Psalms	32

This path is the first manifestation, and as such partakes of the perfection of Kether and Chokmah. It is a path for ensuring something is absolutely right, and for realising your own genius and expressing it.

There is a diamond-like clarity on this path, which rises above disparity to the higher unity and interconnectedness of life. From this perspective this path might equally be called the path of the mystic, as it can engender profound mystical states.

There can be a tendency to lose the self on this path, and it is important to remember that as long as you are in human form, the self has a role as a gateway to the rest of the world.

CHAPTER 5

Contemplations

To work magick with the Qabalah, you need to fully immerse yourself in it. This means spending time meditating on the concepts, contemplating the mysteries and connections, and coming to appreciate how it all applies to you. The Yale Librarian Rutherford D Rodgers said of the modern age, *"We're drowning in information, and starved of knowledge."* This would be very true of the Qabalah if all you do is read about it! Whilst you do need to read about the concepts to find out about them, if that is all you do, you will drown in a morass of information. That information needs to be turned into knowledge, and this is done through action – transforming facts into experiences which give understanding. To appreciate and benefit from the Qabalah, you have to practice it, and then you will find the Four Worlds opening up to you, and your path up the Tree of Life will shine like a golden thread.

As we exist in Malkuth, on the elemental plane, we will begin in Malkuth and work up the Tree, building on the foundations as we go. For these contemplations, make yourself comfortable in a room where you will not be disturbed, and allow yourself a reasonable period of time, preferably no less than quarter of an hour. Close your eyes, and work through the contemplation. You should sit with your back straight, either on a chair or the floor.

You may find it useful to record the contemplations and play them to yourself. If you do this, allow time between each paragraph when recording so you do not hurry through and miss the benefits of the material.

Malkuth

Incense: Burn patchouli or vetivert.

You see a beautiful young woman in a green robe, crowned and with a gossamer thin green veil obscuring her face. She stands between two pillars, a black one on her right and a white one on her left. She tells you she is the Gate, and looks at you expectantly. You ponder this and ask her which gate is she? She replies that she is the gate of death, the gate of prayer, the gate of justice, the gate of tears and the gate of the garden of Eden.

The woman speaks again and tells you that she is the virgin and the bride, the queen and the mother. She is the unreflecting mirror and the lower crown. The word crown makes you study the crown she is wearing in more detail, and you realise it has something written on it. The word V.I.T.R.I.O.L. is written on the crown, the alchemical formula of Visita Interiora Terrae Rectificando Invenies Occultum Lapidem, or visit the interior of the earth and there by rectification find the hidden stone. This is the first part of the journey of Malkuth, inside the earth which is also your body, to discover the hidden stone. This is the philosopher's stone, the vessel of perfection, which is also the divine spark within you. The light of the hidden stone illuminates the path for you to manifest that perfection as you realise more of your potential and evolve, becoming all you can be.

The woman removes her veil, revealing her true beauty, and you realise that she is nature, the mother of all living things. With this realisation, she smiles at you, and stands to one side, gesturing that you should walk between the pillars.

Yesod

Incense: Burn camphor or jasmine.

You see a beautiful naked young man with well toned muscles which hint at great strength. He stands between two pillars, a black one on his right and a white one on his left. He tells you he is the pillar connecting heaven and earth and waits while you consider this. He continues that he is the seal of truth which is the all. When you appreciate this, you will know that righteousness is the foundation of the world.

The man tells you that you are at the lower end of the heavens, and that you must harness your creative power to utilise the life of the worlds. You consider the nature of power, and as you do the man says the word Elohim to you. You consider gods, and realise that you will need to evaluate and re-evaluate your perception of deity and relationship with the divine constantly as you climb up the Tree.

The man nods, and then his features and figure shifts and he becomes a beautiful woman. You realise that in the realm of the moon things can change at any time, and may not always be what they seem. With a satisfied nod, she steps to one side and indicates with a gesture that you should walk between the pillars.

Hod

Incense: Burn lavender, lime or storax

You see a beautiful naked hermaphrodite, with an androgynous face, breasts and a penis, standing between two pillars, a black one on the right and a white one on the left. The hermaphrodite tells you the righteous person is one who has conquered illusions and accepted truth.

From this comes the sincerity that characterises the true seeker on the path of wisdom.

The hermaphrodite continues, telling you that in splendour there is also submission. There is a time to be passive and a time to be active; the key is knowing when each is. You realise that prayer is a form of submission, by accepting alignment to the creative divine. As you consider this, the word AZOTH appears in front of you in the air in flaming orange letters. You remember that Azoth is the alchemical fluid, the essence of life that permeates everything and acts as a catalyst for change and growth towards perfection.

The hermaphrodite nods and reminds you that steadfastness is vital when everything around you is in flux. With a nod, the hermaphrodite steps to one side and indicates with a gesture that you should walk between the pillars.

Netzach

Incense: Burn sandalwood or rose

You see a stunningly beautiful and disturbingly sexy mature woman in her late thirties, standing between two pillars, a black one on the right and a white one on the left. She tells you that to experience eternity you need to appreciate the lasting endurance of god, within and without. The persistence of the seeker for the divine is only matched by, and sometimes equal to, the persistence of love expressing itself.

She tells you that she is agapé and she is storge, she is philia and she is eros. Where there is love or the inspiration produced by love, she is. She is the confidence that stems from knowing you love and are loved. She is also the firmness that will ensure victory by not being distracted or dissuaded from the goals ahead. You remember the saying that love is the strongest force in the universe, and appreciate that without it you will not progress on your path. You need to love yourself, love others, and love the world.

The woman smiles with encouragement as you realise this, and steps aside, permitting you to walk forward between the pillars.

Tiphereth

Incense: Burn frankincense, juniper or rosemary

You see a handsome mature man standing in a green robe with a golden crown on his head, standing between two pillars, a black one on the right and a white one on the left. He fixes you with a serious gaze and announces that he is the Lesser Countenance, the reflecting mirror. He is the clemency of compassion and reconciliation.

He explains that he is the fortunate groom of the bride you have already met, and you realise his robe is the same green that you saw on the veiled women in Malkuth. A groom (or bride) is a blessed holy one when his partner shares his dreams and there is harmony between them. For love will not stand in the way of growth, it will rather nurture it and help produce the greater harmony. That is one of the mysteries expressed by the formula of Yeheshuah (IHShVH).

As he speaks he turns into a beautiful young boy of about seven or eight years old. He crown disappears and his robe shrinks with him, and you realise that he is the son, as Malkuth was the daughter. He is the promise, within him is the potential that will manifest as the king. The boy nods at you and stands aside, gesturing that you should walk between the pillars.

Geburah

Incense: Burn basil, dragon's blood or opoponax

You see a mighty warrior garbed in crimson red armed with a sword and spear, standing in a chariot pulled by two horses, a black one on his right and a white one on the left. The horses' colours match the pillars the chariot stands between, with a black pillar on his right and a white pillar on his left.

The warrior booms at you that fear is part of everyone, and should be welcomed as a friend that warns or challenges you, giving you strength not weakness. How you deal with fear will determine if you act in courage or terror. A courageous person uses their fear and makes it part of their power, aided by the desire for balance and justice.

He speaks again, and declares O star of strength, you are strong to eternity, O lord. You realise he is declaring the expansion of the formula of Agla, and as you do so you see the letters of this name in red fire in front of you. The warrior pulls his chariot to one side so the space between the pillars is empty. At a nod from the warrior, you walk through the fiery name and between the pillars.

Chesed

Incense: Burn cedar or hyssop

You see a mighty figure of a king, robed in sapphire blue with a golden crown, sitting on a marble throne. On his right is a black pillar and on his left is a white pillar. The king radiates power and benevolence, his majesty obviously an inherent part of his being. In his right hand he holds an orb and in his left a sceptre. You realise that he is the successful ruler of his world.

Compassion, like mercy, are easy to express when you are in a state of grace, he tells you. It is when you are feeling out of balance, or out of love, that expressing these qualities shows real glory.

Wear the robe of glory, he instructs you, and as he does so, you see a white glow form around you. You vibrate the divine name Yahveh, and both the robe and you seem to become more solid. Simultaneously the throne fades away and the king steps aside, leaving the passage between the pillars free. Confidently you step through them.

Binah

Incense: Burn myrrh

You see a beautiful mature woman in her forties, wearing a simple black robe, standing between two pillars. On her right is a black pillar and on her left is a white pillar. Her face shines on the right with an inner radiance and seems to be veiled in shadow on the left, and you realise that she is both the bright fertile mother and also the dark sterile mother. Although she is standing, you see a throne behind her made from a single piece of star sapphire, deep blue with an inner star shining bright.

To enter the palace you must cross the great sea, she tells you. That sea manifests in many ways, and more than once. To cross it you must combine everything you have learned and experienced in the seven Sephiroth below. Entering the supernal realm is a step into the unknown, and must be done with conviction and joy.

You know that this beautiful woman is the Shekinah, the goddess who dwells in all of us, and you bow out of respect to her. Smiling, she steps aside, and this time the throne remains between the pillars. She points at the throne, and you step forward and sit on the throne, and feel the divine presence fill your entire being.

Chokmah

Incense: Burn galbanum or musk

You see a mature and strong bearded man in a grey robe standing between two pillars, black on his right and white on his left. Between the pillars you make out the vastness of space, which simultaneously seems to be a cubic room. You blink as the vision switches between the two views, and they seem to overlay each other, and you realise that this is the inner chamber.

The man tells you he is the only begotten son, the first-born of Elohim. The power of Tetragrammaton passes through him, for he is the Yod of Tetragrammaton, the revelation of what is to come. The power of his presence fills you, and you are awestruck by the potency of the divine force all around you.

The man gestures between the pillars, and you stand between them. As you do so you feel your being expanding, and filling the inner chamber, becoming part of the vastness of space there in the cosmic cube.

Kether

Incense: Burn almond or ambergris

You find yourself standing between the two pillars, with the black pillar on your right side and the white pillar on your left side. In front of you an endless sea seems to stretch on for eternity. From the sea you see a giant bearded head in profile, its right side towards you, rising. The head is surrounded by brilliant white light, which surround it like veils.

Phrases fill the air around you, hinting at the awesome nature in front of you, ancient of days, inscrutable height, the most high, the hidden light, the head that is not, the vast countenance, the white head that is the profuse giver. With each title you feel the energy around you growing stronger and stronger until you feel like you are going to explode.

There is a discharge of energy which fills your entire being, and you feel like you are the point within the circle. You look around and find yourself back in front of the beautiful veiled woman you encountered in Malkuth. She looks different now, or perhaps it is that you see her differently, for you realise that she is the younger version of the woman you encountered in Binah. She smiles and reminds you that Kether is in Malkuth, and Malkuth in Kether, but after a different fashion.

CHAPTER 6

The Vibratory Formula

The Divine Names are considered incredibly powerful, and even simply speaking them may begin processes of change. However the words of power in Qabalah are usually vibrated rather than being spoken. This means that when you pronounce Divine Names, or the names of Archangels, Angels or Heavens, they should be vibrated. When you vibrate a name you must breathe properly. This may sound obvious, but the natural tendency is to breathe shallow breaths.

To vibrate a word you need to breathe from your diaphragm, and prolong the duration of the syllables. You will know when you have found the right pitch for your vibrations, as you will literally feel your rib-cage, and possibly the rest of your body, vibrate with the power of the word you are uttering.

This does not mean that you have to shout or be very loud; the important thing is to find the right pitch for you which causes an internal vibration. Vibration is not a contest; it is an alignment with particular flows of energy by pronouncing the formulae of that flow. The pitch varies from person to person, and requires no musical knowledge or ability.

The benefit of vibrating or intoning words is that we all have a voice, and by using it we are not only projecting our intent from ourselves into the universe, but we are also adding energy to that intent, for sound is energy. We are also literally *'giving voice'* to ourselves, empowering our actions by making our presence felt. Vibration of divine names and other words of power gives us access to energy immediately without the need for preparation, and from this perspective it is a very powerful way to generate energy quickly if you need to. E.g., if you needed to be confident before a meeting, you could quietly vibrate the divine name of Geburah (if you could find a suitable discrete spot), or before an exam you could vibrate the divine name of Hod. The possibilities are manifold once you realise the simple effectiveness of this technique for enhancing situations.

Regular use of the voice to vibrate words has the additional effect of focusing our attention on what is important. If you practice the vibratory formula every day, you will notice yourself questioning those little things you do which no longer have value, and which only serve to tie up energy and hold you back. Your baggage is *'shaken free'* by the power of your voice and the vibration of your body, and it can then be released and the energy directed into your growth, moving you further on your path to perfection.

The Practice

Before you inhale to pronounce the words, see the name in the air in front of you in its appropriate Sephirotic colour. It is preferable to see the name written in Hebrew, remembering that Hebrew is written right to left, but if you find this too difficult see the name in the Roman alphabet.

In addition to focusing your breath, you also need to focus your mind. When you inhale the breath before vibrating the words of power, you should see the breath also being the Sephirotic colour. Feel the energy of the Sephira entering your body and suffusing your being.

You should now feel energised, as if your body has grown in size and strength, and be aware that your aura is now suffused with the Sephirotic colour. You may even see a faint haze of the colour around yourself, at the edge of your aura. Feel your power focused in your heart, ready to be released on your exhalation.

Now breathe out, and on the exhalation vibrate the divine name. Be aware of the increase in magical charge around you as the power of your intent coupled with that of the divine name surrounds you and energises your environment, filling it like a cup ready to drink when you need to draw on the power.

When you vibrate words, your spine should be straight, so it is preferable to either be standing up, or sitting in a straight-backed chair or cross-legged on the floor.

E.g. if you were vibrating the Divine Name of Yesod, Shaddai, you would see the name and the inhaled air being silver in colour, as the Sephirotic colour of Yesod. However if you were vibrating Eheieh, the Divine Name of Kether, the name and breath would be brilliant white.

By breathing properly and vibrating words, and focusing your mind through the use of the correct colours, you will notice it is easier to achieve altered states of consciousness. You will be more aware of both the energy you generate, and also the energies around you. Try with the Tetragrammaton as Yah-veh (IHVH), seeing the name and the air you inhale as a pure soft grey. Practice until you can feel your body vibrating as you intone the syllables, drawing them out so that each syllable takes 5-10 seconds to vibrate.

This practice should be performed for each of the Sephira on the Tree in turn, to help attune you to their energy. It can also be used with appropriate divine names before performing meditations and pathworkings to help focus and empower you for the work to come. Vibration is also used with another very powerful technique, *Yechudim*, or Unification of the Divine Names.

Sephira	Divine Name	Pronunciation
Kether	Eheieh	E-hay-ya
Chokmah	Yah	Yah
Binah	Yahveh	Yah-veh
Daath	Ruach haQadosh	Roo-ack ha Ka-dosh
Chesed	El	El
Geburah	Elohim Givor	El-o-heem Gi-vor
Tiphereth	Eloah	El-o-ah
Netzach	Yahveh Zavaot	Yah-veh Za-vay-ot
Hod	Elohim Zavaot	El-o-heem Za-vay-ot
Yesod	Shaddai	Sha-dye
Malkuth	Adonai Melekh	Ah-don-i Mel-ek

CHAPTER 7

The Divine Names

"The most Learned Hebrew Qabalists, have Received the ten principal & most sacred names of God, as certain Divine powers, which by ten numerations (called Sephiroth) as it were instruments of examples of the Archetype have influence on all things Created (by a certain Order) from the High things even to the Lord, for first they have immediate Influence on the nine orders of Angels & Choirs of Blessed Souls, & by them into the Celestial Spheres, planets & men, by which Sephiroth, everything receiveth power & virtues &c."[20]

This passage demonstrates the supreme importance of the Divine Names in Qabalah as expressions of the ultimate creative essence. The appropriate Divine Names should be used for any Sephirotic work, as representing the logos of the energy. Sustained vibration of the Divine Name acts as a focus, automatically tuning your work into the correct energy.

The Divine Names are used for empowerment both in spoken and written form. When vibrated they form the basis for focusing spiritual energy, be it for conjuration, healing, prayer, physical results, transformation or any other purpose. Likewise when written they may form the basis of magick circles, amulets and talismans. Traditionally

---

[20] Sloane MS 3825.

Divine Names are essential for Qabalistic practices involving any form of creation.

Whenever a divine name is used, whether it is vibrated or written, it should always be seen in flames of a colour appropriate to the Sephira. There are two terms used in Qabalistic texts with regard to divine names and their use, which are *chakikah* (*'engraving'*) and *chatzivah* (*'hewing'* or *'carving'*).

Sephira	Divine Name	Hebrew	Transliteration	English
Kether	Eheieh	אהיה	AHIH	I am
Chokmah	Yah	יה	IH	God
Binah	Yahveh	יהוה	IHVH	Lord
Daath	Ruach ha-Qadosh	רואח הקדש	RVACh HQDSh	Spirit of Holiness
Chesed	El	אל	AL	God
Geburah	Elohim Givor	אלהימגיבור	ALHIM GIBVR	Strong Gods
Tiphereth	Eloah	אלוה	ALVH	God
Netzach	Yahveh Zavaot	יהוהצבאות	IHVH TzBAVTh	Lord of Hosts
Hod	Elohim Zavaot	אלהימצבאות	ALHIM TzBAVTh	Gods of Hosts
Yesod	Shaddai	שדי	ShDI	Almighty
Malkuth	Adonai Melekh	אדנימלכ	ADNI MLK	Lord King

Engraving refers to the process of fixing the image in the mind's eye so it is firm and does not waver or change shape or colour. The phrase *"burned in my thoughts"* is a good analogy to this, for you literally engrave the image in your mind. When you do this you see the image with certainty, it is not simply visualisation.

Carving or hewing refers to the removal of unwanted aspects of the image you are seeing. So for instance if you were seeing letters you remove all other imagery leaving a blank wall of colour behind it. The analogy here is to hewing a gemstone out of the surrounding matrix of rock, and chipping away any extraneous bits of material to leave the desired gem.

The Divine Names used for Tiphereth (*Eloah*) and Yesod (*Shaddai*), are the older names, rather than the later names which have been popularised in modern writings (*Yahveh Eloah va-Daath* and *Shaddai El Chai*).

CHAPTER 8

Unification of the Divine Names

A very good meditation technique that can produce many insights and powerful meditative experiences is called *Yichudim* (*'unification'*). Unification has been used by Qabalists for many centuries and is very good for elevating the consciousness towards the divine. For this reason, the technique is often used as the opening component for prayer to assist in directing the prayer all the way up the Tree of Life.

The technique is straightforward, as most powerful techniques are, and essentially involves the unification of Divine Names, their pronunciation, and then meditating on them. This can be performed at any time and in any place, though you will also benefit from using unification within a Sephira (i.e. a Sephirotic temple), and the practice may also be used when you wish to combine the energies of two Sephiroth which have a path connecting them, rather than just using one.

This technique requires you to see complex images, i.e. a sequence of Hebrew letters for a sustained period of time, and may require some practice to use effectively.

There are two easy ways of performing this technique which do not require you to be fluent in Hebrew, both of which we will explore. These are simply to combine the Divine Names by putting alternate letters, or the slightly more complex spelling the letters of each name in full, and then combining them.

Obviously this technique only works when the Divine Names of the two Sephiroth you seek to unite have an equal number of letters, or the higher Sephira has one more letter than the lower. This is because the first letter will always be the first letter of the Divine Name for the highest Sephira. To this end, we have included some alternative Divine Names from Qabalistic texts for the Sephiroth to enable this technique to be used right across the Tree.

It should be noted that as this technique is sometimes performed within the Sephira, Daath is not included as it does not have a temple in the same way, nor are its energies of quite the same nature.

Simple Unification

To illustrate the principle of simple unification, we will use the Sephiroth of Tiphereth and Yesod as an example.

If you wanted to work with the combined energies of Tiphereth and Yesod (Sun and Moon), you would combine the letters of their respective Divine Names, and then vibrate and see the unified name. However the difficult part comes in seeing the images of the Hebrew, for the letters should be seen in the appropriate colours. To illustrate:

- The respective Divine Names for Tiphereth and Yesod are Eloah (ALVH) and El Chi (ALChI).
- The letters are combined in turn, i.e. the first letter of Eloah, then the first letter of El Chi, then the second letter of each, to the last letters.
- As each extra letter is seen, the unified name is built up.
- This then gives a unified name of AALLVChHI
- The letters are then vibrated in turn to give the whole unified name.

- This would be seen (right to left obviously) with the letters alternately gold and silver, with the letters taken from Eloah being gold, and those from El Chi being silver.
- The unified name would thus be seen as Aleph (gold), Aleph (silver), Lamed (gold), Lamed (silver), Vav (gold), Cheth (silver), Heh (gold), Yod (silver).

Complex Unification

The process of complex unification is carried out in the same manner as Simple Unification, with the difference that the divine names are each vibrated in full first, with each letter of each name being spelt in full. For the same example of the unification of Tiphereth and Yesod this would be:

- Aleph Lamed Peh (A), Lamed Mem Daleth (L), Vav Vav (V), Heh Heh (H), this being Eloah with each letter spelt and vibrated in full.
- Then the same for El Chi, i.e. Aleph Lamed Peh (A), Lamed Mem Daleth (L), Cheth Yod Tav (Ch), Yod Vav Daleth (I).
- The unified name is then created in the same manner as for the Simple Unification, from the point of seeing each letter in turn and then vibrating them in sequence.
- So as each letter is vibrated and seen, the unified name is built up, giving a unified name of AALLVChHI
- This would be seen (right to left obviously) with the letters alternately gold and silver, with the letters taken from Eloah being gold, and those from El Chi being silver.
- The unified name would thus be seen as Aleph (gold), Aleph (silver), Lamed (gold), Lamed (silver), Vav (gold), Cheth (silver), Heh (gold), Yod (silver).

The Divine Names for Unification

Sephira	Divine Name	Letters	Colour	Notes
Kether	Eheieh	AHIH	White	
Chokmah	Yah Ab	IH AB	Grey	Ab means *Father*, a title used for Chokmah
Binah	Yahveh	IHVH	Black	
Chesed	Elon	ALVN	Blue	Elon is a form of Elion, meaning *Highest God*, and used as a Divine Name for Chesed
Geburah	Agla	AGLA	Red	
Tiphereth	Eloah	ALVH	Gold	
Netzach	Owlam	OVLM	Green	Owlam means *Eternity*, a title of Netzach
Hod	Elohim	ALIM	Orange	This is the shortened form of the name Elohim (*Gods*), used in the Divine Name of Hod and all of the Sephiroth on this pillar
Yesod	El Chi	AL ChI	Silver	El Chi means *Everliving God*, and is used as a Divine Name for Yesod
Malkuth	Adonai	ADNI	Brown	Adonai is used in both the Divine Names for Malkuth, Adonai Melekh and Adona ha-Aretz

Unification up the Tree

For practices like prayer and cultivating Ruach HaQadosh, you may wish to work up the Tree of Life systematically through the Sephiroth, as was described by great Qabalists of the past. This is essentially an ascent up the path of the Lightning Flash.

Each combination of Sephiroth is unified in turn, working up the Tree. Thus you would first unify the Divine Names of Malkuth and Yesod, and then when you had done this to your satisfaction, you would move on to unify the Divine Names of Yesod and Hod. This process is then repeated moving up the Tree in ascending order through the Sephiroth, so that the final unification would be for the Divine Names of Chokmah and Kether.

The sequence is illustrated in the table below:

Ascent	Unified Name	Letter Colours (Alternate)
Malkuth-Yesod	AALDChNII	Silver & Brown
Yesod-Hod	AALLIChMI	Orange & Silver
Hod-Netzach	OAVLLIMM	Green & Orange
Netzach-Tiphereth	AOLVVLHM	Gold & Green
Tiphereth-Geburah	AAGLLVAH	Red & Gold
Geburah-Chesed	AALGVLNA	Blue & Red
Chesed-Binah	IAHLVVHN	Black & Blue
Binah-Chokmah	IIHHAVBH	Grey & Black
Chokmah-Kether	AIHHIAHB	White & Grey

CHAPTER 9

The Archangels

"First they be no Gods but most perfect Creatures produced by the omnipotent hand of God for that unity simplicity and independence be most perfect attribute."[21]

The archangels are the active powers who act as lenses for the divine emanations which make up the Tree, like the rays of colour light dividing through a prism from the original divine white light. They are attributed to the second World on the Tree, that of Briah (the Creative World). The archangels are one of the keys to working with the Qabalah, as they help make the unknowable knowable. The Archangels are specialized functionaries, each fulfilling their function within the scheme of the universe. It is important that you do not underestimate the power of archangels and their ability to create change and direct energy towards a particular end. Working with the Archangels will help keep you very focused on your path, and ensure you do not stray into too many bad habits.

There are a number of ways of grouping the archangels, including the seven who stand in the presence of God (planetary) and the four archangels of the directions or elements. The four archangels of the lower elemental planetary forces, i.e. Gabriel, Raphael, Uriel and Michael, have been grouped together for rites and spells for at least the last fifteen hundred years. Considering this, the Jewish protective

[21] *Treatise of Angels*, Salkeld, C17th.

prayer of *Kriat Shema al ha-Mitah*, for guarding a person during their sleep, shows its Qabalistic roots. The prayer for protection, which was adapted by the Golden Dawn for the Lesser Banishing Ritual of the Pentagram, declares:

In the name of Adonai the God of Israel:
May the angel Michael be at my right,
And the angel Gabriel be at my left;
And in front of me the angel Uriel;
And behind me the angel Raphael;
And above my head the Shekinah.

The symbolism is clear in the use of the divine name of Adonai, which is specifically associated with Malkuth, followed by the four archangels of the Sephiroth from Yesod to Tiphereth, and finally the Shekinah who can be seen as both the Middle Pillar and Binah.

Over the years we have noticed an absence of material on the zodiacal archangels, though they were seen in the grimoires, from *Liber Juratus* in the thirteenth century onwards, through the writings of Renaissance magicians such as Cornelius Agrippa and Thomas Rudd. As a result of our own work and research, particularly in grimoires and Qabalistic works of sixteenth and seventeenth century Europe, we have provided descriptions of the traditional attributions and appearances of these archangels for use. As far as we know this is the first time that this information has been made generally available.

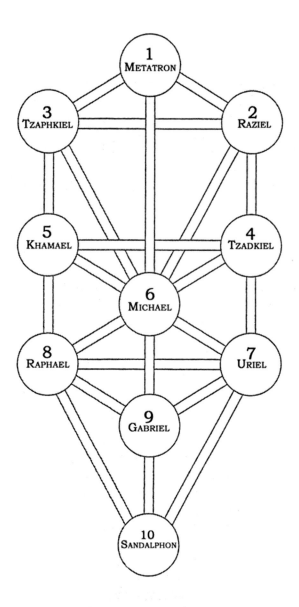

THE ARCHANGELS OF THE SEPHIROTH

Metatron (MTTRVN)

Metatron (or Methratron or Mitthratron) is the *'Voice of God'*. The force of God's voice is perceived as being too great for any living being, that it would destroy them through its power. Hence Metatron acts as the voice of God, enabling that force to be expressed in a manner that does not overcome. Enoch is said to have become Metatron, raised to the highest rank due to his piety, becoming transformed into a being of pure fire. He is described as the Prince of the Divine Countenance (*Malach ha-Panim*) or Angel of the Divine Countenance (*Sar ha-Panim*).

Address:

O thou Prince of the Divine Countenance
Who stands at the right hand of the Ancient of Days
Thou who art accompanied by fire stones and hailstones on your right
And wings of storm and strength of tempest on your left
You hold the Throne of Glory in a multitude of wings
Uttering the divine words of the Shemhamphorash

Vision:

You see a huge male figure sitting on a giant throne, made of gleaming white marble. He is a beautifully proportioned young man, wearing a brilliant white robe, and whenever he moves rainbows fill the air around him. The light shining from his face is so brilliant that it is impossible to see his features clearly, but you can just make out a golden crown on his head. As you gaze upon his form, the air around you is filled with the flapping of numerous wings, which contrasts with the peaceful silence you feel in your mind.

Raziel (RTzIAL)

Raziel means *'Herald of God'*. As the archangel associated with wisdom (Chokmah), we can see why Raziel is given as one of the two possible Archangels who transmitted knowledge of the Kabbalah to Adam. He is also known as *Galizur* (*'Revealer of the Rock'*), and was said to protect the other angels from the fiery breath of the Chaioth ha Qadosh with his wings.

Address:

> *O thou Keeper of Divine Secrets*
> *Revealer of the Rock*
> *Thou who spread your protective wings over the angels*
> *To protect them from the fiery breath of the Chaioth ha Qadosh*
> *You bestow the wisdom of the mysteries*
> *Distributing the blessings of the Shekinah*

Vision:

You see a beautiful male figure standing on a pinnacle of rock, framed by the night sky behind him. He has a beautiful and wise face, and wears a soft grey tunic and sandals. His white wings stretch out into the heavens, and at their tips you see points of light. Stars seem to twinkle and shine about his head as he moves, like an ever-changing diadem of constellations. As you gaze upon Raziel, you feel your mind expanding, and feel a oneness with the vastness of space that surrounds you.

Tzaphkiel (TzPhKIAL)

Tzaphkiel means *'Beholder of God'*, though he is also sometimes called as Jophiel (*'Beauty of God'*). Tzaphkiel is one of the seven Archangels who stand in the presence of God. He is known as the

Angel of Paradise because of his role in the Garden of Eden, and in modern times is the patron of all those who fight pollution and love and protect nature. He is also the patron of artists, bringing illumination and inspiration to those who seek to create beauty in the world. He is the first angel mentioned in the Bible, though not by name, being the guardian of the Tree of Life, and it was he who drove Adam and Eve from the Garden of Eden after they had eaten the forbidden apple, and bars the return of man, standing at the gates bearing the flaming sword.

Address:

> O thou beholder of God
> Bearer of the flaming sword who guards the portals of Eden
> Your flame brings illumination and inspiration to all who see you
> And your beauty brings peace to those who call you
> You stand poised in the eternal now
> Balanced between force and form

Vision:

You see an almost painfully beautiful male angel standing on a dune of white sand. He is wearing a black tunic, with white wings, and he bears a flaming sword in his right hand. His beauty is captivating, and the patterns of shadow and light made on his face by the flames of his sword only serve to highlight his beauty further.

As you look upon Tzaphkiel, you feel a subtle pressure on your skin all over, making you very aware of the boundaries of your body. Concentrate on this sensation and push it outwards, so it moves to the edge of your aura.

Anpiel (AaNPIAL)

We would suggest that the angel Anpiel is probably the most appropriate archangel to work with for Daath. The description and symbolism attributed to him in chapter 23 of the *Hekhalot Rabbati* (*'Greater Palaces'*) clearly indicate this role for him.

> *"Anpiel YVY, an angel whose name is uttered before the Throne of Glory three times each day. Praised from the day that the world was created until now. And why? Because the Ring containing the seal of heaven and earth is given over into his hand. When all on high see him, they bow, fall on their faces, and prostrate themselves before him. This is not true, however, of those on the highest level."* [22]

This clearly suggests his position is in Daath. Not only does he bear the Ring which symbolises the six Sephiroth of Construction in his hand, suggesting he is above them (i.e. above Chesed), but those on the highest level (i.e. the Supernal Triad) do not prostrate themselves. Thus he is clearly placed between the bottom of the Supernals (Binah) and top of the Sephiroth of Construction (Chesed). Between Binah and Chesed is Daath.

> *"And why is he more beloved than all the guardians of the six doors of the Chambers. This is because he opens the door of the Seventh Chamber."* [23]

This is further reinforced by two more quotes in the same verse of the *Greater Hekhalot*. As the opener of the seventh door, that of Binah, he is clearly above Chesed but below Binah, so in the Abyss, i.e. at Daath. He is also described as having the foliage of crowns upon crowns on his head. The Supernal Triad are all described as being crowns, not just Kether (Crown), and again as being just above his head, this places him at Daath.

> *"Why is he called Anpiel? It is because of the foliage [Anaph] of crowns upon crowns that is on his head."* [24]

---

[22] *Hekhalot Rabbati 23.*

[23] *Hekhalot Rabbati 23.*

[24] *Hekhalot Rabbati 23.*

Address:

O thou ring bearing guardian of the heavens
Thou who opens the door to the seventh chamber
Whose heads is graced with the foliage of crowns
And who stand before the Bridal Chamber
You stand in the hidden space
In the light of the midnight sun

Vision:

You see a tall and beautiful angel wearing a lavender robe and a foliate crown on his head standing in space. Light seems to shine from every pore of his body. Behind him you see a black sun, and the black light from it radiates out behind Anpiel, and contrasts his pale light, highlighting his fine features. As you watch him, he reaches out and grabs a floating leaf from space in front of himself and places it in his crown. You realise this was a prayer which he has gathered to take into the divine presence and consider the balance inherent in his appearance and nature, a balance you too can achieve through your thoughts and actions.

Tzadkiel (TzDQIAL)

Tzadkiel, is also known as Zadkiel, Satqiel, Zedkiel and Zachiel, whose name means *'Righteousness of God'*. He is the archangel of benevolence, memory and mercy, and he is often depicted with a dagger in his hand, representing the two-edged power of the intellect. Tzadkiel is a comforter, and he is associated with invocation and prayer. He is hence the archangel to help overcome despondency, and to help you forgive others for their negative deeds.

Through prayer and invocation he is also a channel to help you attune yourself with divinity in the way you perceive and experience it. As archangel of Jupiter, Tzadkiel can also be appealed to for help with financial matters and for achieving justice in a situation.

Address:

O thou righteous and benevolent power
Who wields the dagger of discrimination and duty
You offer mercy from strength
Your battle standard inspires all to victory
Over themselves as well as their adversities
Through compassionate potency

Vision:

You see a beautiful slender angel wearing a blue tunic standing in front of a waterfall. He holds a dagger in his left hand and a large cut sapphire in his right hand. The tips of his wings seem razor sharp, as if they are feather daggers. As you gaze at the sapphire you become fascinated by its intense blue colour, first like the sea, and then like a clear sky. As you look more closely you see a shape in the sapphire, and realise it has a throne shaped within its facets. The power emanating from the sapphire draws your attention back to Tzadkiel, and you become aware of his role in mediating forces of change, and your own ability to change.

Khamael (KhMAL)

Khamael (or Samael or Camael) is one of the seven Archangels who stand in the presence of god, whose name means 'he who sees God'. His name is reflected in the fact that he is sometimes described as being covered with eyes. Khamael is a warrior who represents divine justice. Khamael is the ideal angel to call upon to help you take personal responsibility and to develop self-confidence. He will help you deal with the consequences of your actions and to find justice, but only if you stick to the truth. hamael is said to grant invisibility, and rules over martial qualities like power and invincibility. He is the angel who guards the gates of heaven, chief of the twelve thousand fiery Angels of destruction who guard the gates. Khamael is also the angel who holds

Leviathan in check until Judgement Day, when he will swallow the souls of sinners. Other duties of Khamael are as patron Angel of all those who love God, governing the heavenly singing, and to bring the gift of godliness to mankind, helping them find the holiness that exists within but is rarely fully released.

Address:

O thou who see God
Invincible warrior and bestower of divine justice
You who take the souls of men
From death to transformation
You open the inner paths to holiness and perfection
Making visible the hidden ways within

Vision:

You see a stern angelic figure in a scarlet tunic with an open-faced iron helmet and a green breastplate and plates of armour. Fiery red hair curls out underneath the bottom of his helmet. He carries a large sword in his right hand, and his large green wings extend out behind him. Khamael turns his sword so you can only see its edge, and you realise that a change in perspective can make things much clearer or more obscure. He turns the sword again so the flat of the blade faces you, and you see your reflection in the blade.

Michael (MIKAL)

Michael means 'He who is like God', and he was the first angel created, and is often seen as the leader of the angels. Michael helps those who call him to achieve goals and destinies. Amongst the achievements especially sacred to Michael are marriage and music. If you are seeking to achieve a legitimate goal, or in need of protection, Michael is the angel you should call to, as he is the defender of the just and is also known as the Merciful Angel.

Michael appears a number of times in the Bible. Michael was the archangel who appeared to Moses as the fire in the burning bush. He also rescued Daniel from the lion's den and informed Mary of her approaching death. Michael appears in Revelations as the leader of the celestial host that defeats the antichrist.

Address:

> O thou who art like God
> Beautiful and mighty fire of perfection
> In your mercy you defend the just
> And lead the celestial hordes of angels
> From your sword to the triangle
> You control all spirits and beings

Vision:

You see a tall and well-built beautiful angel, wearing a golden tunic. An aura of majesty surrounds him, and light seems to emanate from every part of his body. He wields a lance in his right hand and a set of scales in his left hand. Simply seeing him makes you feel more positive and dynamic, and his presence drives all negativity from you, giving you the determination to achieve the goals you had in mind.

Uriel (AVRIAL)

Uriel, (or Auriel or Oriel) means 'Light of God', and he is often depicted with a flame or lamp in his hands. He is the Archangel of peace and salvation, embodying the power of light as illumination and spiritual passion. Uriel is associated with magical power, and the application of force. As such he is the angel to help cause a positive breaking of bonds when needed and overcoming inertia, being able to go with the flow of the 'winds of change'. He is also the patron of astrology and has been linked strongly with electricity.

Uriel is credited with being the angel who gave alchemy and the Qabalah to man. As one of the most powerful Archangels, Uriel is said to be the bearer of the keys to hell, standing as guardian to that infernal realm.

Address:

> O thou Light of God
> Bearing the lamp of peace in your hands
> Thou are the power of illumination
> The force of salvation and transformation
> Guardian of the infernal gates
> You bear the keys of light and darkness.

Vision:

You see a beautiful feminine angel wearing an emerald green robe standing in a forest glade. He carries a copper lamp in his left hand, which gives out a subtle yet powerful radiance. In his right hand is a bronze ring with large ornate keys hanging from it. The keys seem to emanate waves of heat and cold simultaneously, making you think of how extremes of any type can be problematic. Uriel waves his lamp and the rays of light from it blow over you like a wind, dispelling all other sensations, and leaving you feeling refreshed and invigorated.

Raphael (RPhAL)

Raphael means 'Healer of God', and he is the archangel charged with healing mankind and the earth. Raphael is also the patron of travellers, often being depicted with a pilgrim's staff, and he protects those on journeys, especially air travel. As well as protecting travellers, Raphael's special charges are the young and innocent. Raphael is the archangel of knowledge and communication, and may be called to help with any related areas, such as improving your memory, learning languages, exams, dealing with bureaucracy and business matters.

Raphael was said to have healed the earth after the Flood, and also visited Noah after the Flood to give him a book of medicine, which had belonged to the angel Raziel.

Address:

O thou healer of God
Bestowing protection and knowledge
Thou mighty and benevolent patron
Of all who travel around the earth
In your wisdom
Is all restoration found

Vision:

You see a beautiful, fine-featured angel standing on a hilltop. He wears an orange tunic, and has a staff in his right hand. Around the staff is coiled a snake, with its head resting by his hand. There is an air of serenity about him which fills you, making you feel incredibly calm and lifting your spirits, dispelling any aches or pains your body felt. As you look at him you realise he does not consider anything impossible or accept defeat, and you resolve to emulate his example.

Gabriel (GBRIAL)

Gabriel means *'The Strength of God'*. Gabriel is the angel who usually delivers messages to humanity, embodying the link between man and the universe and the divine as expressed by Yesod. Gabriel first appears in the Old Testament in the book of Daniel. It is Gabriel who first indicates the coming of a messiah to Daniel in this book. Gabriel visited Zachary to tell him his son would be called John (the Baptist) and most famously he told Mary that she was pregnant with Jesus. In Islam Gabriel is also seen as the divine messenger, it was he who delivered the Qur'an to Mohammed. Gabriel is the guide to the inner tides of our unconscious. Gabriel can help with developing the imagination and psychic abilities. He is also associated with domestic matters, especially the development of the home, or finding a new home.

Gabriel can appear as male or female, and may be called to as either. Gabriel often appears carrying a staff topped with lilies, showing his fruitful nature and ability to help you bring plans to fruition.

Address:

> O thou Strength of God
> Messenger divine who inspires and guides
> Providing truth with every utterance
> Thou art the tongue that reveals the holy plan
> Both female and male in turn
> Thou changest with the cycles and seasons

Vision:

You see a beautiful feminine angel wearing a violet robe standing in a field of white lilies. In his left hand he bears a silver cup, and in his right hand a staff topped with lilies. As you gaze at him his face seems to become more masculine, and then the curves soften and it becomes more feminine again. You realise that Gabriel has the ability to become whatever he needs to be to deal with a situation, and know that you can strive for this mutable form too.

Sandalphon (SNDLPhVN)

Sandalphon (also known as Hadraniel, Haviviel and Yagidiel) is thought to be derived from the Greek *synadelphos* meaning 'brother' or 'brotherly one'. In this context he is the brother to Metatron, for Sandalphon transmits the prayers of man to the heavens, and also stands behind the divine throne making garlands or crowns for the head of the most high. These crowns are made from the prayers of the faithful, which Sandalphon has received. In his full glory he is said to be more than five hundred years taller than his brother.

Modern writers often say that Sandalphon means *"the sound of sandals"*. The reason given for this spurious attribution this is that sandals are worn on the feet, connecting us to the ground we walk on, i.e. Malkuth. He is the master of alchemy, the inner alchemy of the soul and the outer process of transformation in nature. Sandalphon is said to differentiate the sex of the embryo in the womb. Sandalphon was also identified with Elijah, who was said to become assumed into Sandalphon on his translation to heaven.

Address:

> O thou mighty Brother of angels
> Standing behind the throne of glory
> Receiving the prayers of the faithful
> Which you have sent from the earth
> Centuries high you stand
> Master of alchemy and nature

Vision:

You see a beautiful androgynous angel, standing in a field of corn. He wears a brown tunic and carries a sheaf of wheat in his right hand, and a poppy in his left hand. The power of the earth seems to emanate from him, waves of strength flowing outwards from him. You realise he is sending you a message of function and beauty, of how inner power can be manifested through actions into tangible results in your environment.

Malchidael (MLKIDAL)

Malchidael (*'king of God'*) is the archangel of Aries. Traditionally he is associated with fertility, both of women and of plants, particularly trees and vegetables.

Vision:

He stands around 3m tall with large white wings behind his back. He has sharp but beautiful features, with flaming red hair and red-brown eyes, is powerfully built, with strong musculature, and wears a red tunic.

Asmodel (AShMODAL)

Asmodel (possibly *'greatness of God'*) is the archangel of Taurus. She is traditionally associated with helping business and transactions to prosper.

Vision:

She stands around 3m tall with large white wings behind her back. She has beautiful strong and full features with brown hair and brown eyes, with a strong build, and wears a red-orange tunic.

Ambriel (AMBRIAL)

Ambriel (possibly *'energy of God'*) is the archangel of Gemini. Traditionally Ambriel is associated with protection when travelling, giving warnings against danger, causing love and facilitating bodily changes (such as weight loss or body-building).

Vision:

He stands around 3m tall with large white wings behind his back. He has beautiful ethereal and fine features, with blonde hair streaked with black and eyes that seem to shift between blue and green. He has a slender build, and wears an orange tunic.

Muriel (MURIAL)

Muriel (*'fragrance of God'*) is the archangel of Cancer. Traditionally she rules over legacies, treasure and treasure-seeking, and speaking, particularly public speaking to audiences.

Vision:

She stands around 3m tall with large white wings behind her back. She has beautiful full features with grey-green hair and deep blue eyes, is voluptuously built, and wears an orange-yellow tunic.

Verchiel (VRKIAL)

Verchiel (*'command of God'*) is the archangel of Leo. Traditionally he has the power to multiply living things and move them, so ideal for spreading crops. He was also said to judge in some manners.

Vision:

He stands around 3m tall with large white wings behind his back. He has beautiful strong and sharp features with red hair and amber eyes, has a strong build, and wears a yellow tunic.

Hamaliel (HMLIAL)

Hamaliel (possibly *'grace of God'*) is the archangel of Virgo. Traditionally she is said to confer health, teach music, logic and ethics, command evil spirits and subvert kingdoms.

Vision:

She stands around 3m tall with large white wings behind her back. She has beautiful ethereal yet full features, with dark brown hair and hazel eyes, with a slender build and wearing a yellow-green tunic.

Zuriel (ZURIAL)

Zuriel (*'rock of God'*) is the archangel of Libra. Traditionally he was said to control the friendship and enmity of all living creatures, so a useful ally for gaining influence.

Vision:

He stands around 3m tall with large white wings behind his back. He has beautiful ethereal features, with piercing grey eyes and blonde hair, has a slender build and wears a green tunic.

Barbiel (BRBIAL)

Barbiel (possibly *'illumination of God'*) is the archangel of Scorpio. Traditionally he was said to bestow knowledge of Theology, Metaphysics and Geomancy, to have power over departed souls, to force demons and men to keep their pacts, and cause suffering and terror where appropriate.

Vision:

She stands around 3m tall with large white wings behind her back. She has beautiful voluptuous features with black hair and electric blue eyes, has a full and voluptuous build, and wears a green-blue tunic.

Adnachiel (ADNKIAL)

Adnachiel (possibly *'happiness of God'*) is the archangel of Sagittarius. He is traditionally able to control the four elements, propagate animals, and lead people from one country to another.

Vision:

He stands around 3m tall with large white wings behind his back. He has beautiful sharp and fine features, with auburn hair and dark brown eyes. He has a slender yet strong build, and wears a blue tunic.

Hanael (HNAL)

Hanael (*'grace of God'*) is the archangel of Capricorn. She is said to confer reason and understanding, give high worldy honours, virtue and worthiness.

Vision:

She stands around 3m tall with large white wings behind her back. She has beautiful full features with brown hair and green eyes, has a full build, and wears a blue-violet tunic.

Cambiel (KAMBIAL)

Cambiel (unknown meaning) is the archangel of Aquarius. Traditionally he was said to teach the mysteries of nature and heaven, what is detrimental to health and how to remain in good health and contented.

He stands around 3m tall with large white wings behind his back. He has beautiful ethereal and strong features with white hair and lavender eyes, has a strong build, and wears a violet tunic.

Barchiel (BRKIAL)

Barchiel (*'the Blessings of God'*) is the archangel of Pisces. Traditionally she was said to compel evil spirits to be subject to men and protect the pious and worthy.

Vision:

She stands around 3m tall with large white wings behind her back. She has beautiful voluptuous features with strawberry blonde hair and grey-green eyes, has a full build and wears a violet-red tunic.

CHAPTER 10

The Angels

The angels are the workforce of the Tree of Life, working under the direction of the archangels to fulfil the divine will. The Orders or Choirs of Angels are the next level of spiritual creatures under the archangels. Each choir of angels also has specific benefits or tasks which they can be called for, to improve areas of life for the magician calling on their aid.

The angels are divided into a hierarchy, which first occurs in the sixth century CE writings of Pseudo-Dionysus the Areopagite (*The Celestial Hierarchy*, c. 500 CE), and matches the division of the Sephiroth into the triads and the Four Worlds. The angels are ideal to call upon for work like talismans and healing, where their numbers ensure you can attract immediate attention.

As with the archangels, a lack of information has pushed us to research Renaissance and earlier texts for information which presents a clearer image of the Orders of Angels. We have provided this information in an effort to make angelic work easier.

Sephira	Angels	Ruler	Called in the Grimoires	Hierarchy
Kether	Chaioth haQadosh	Metatron	Seraphim	Superior
Chokmah	Ophanim	Raziel	Kerubim	Superior
Binah	Aralim	Tzaphkiel	Thrones	Superior
Chesed	Chasmalim	Tzadkiel	Dominations	Middle

Geburah	Seraphim	Kamael	Potestates or Powers	Middle
Tiphereth	Malachim	Michael	Virtues	Middle
Netzach	Elohim	Uriel	Principalities	Inferior
Hod	Bene Elohim	Raphael	Archangels	Inferior
Yesod	Kerubim	Gabriel	Angels	Inferior
Malkuth	Ashim	Sandalphon	Blessed Souls	-

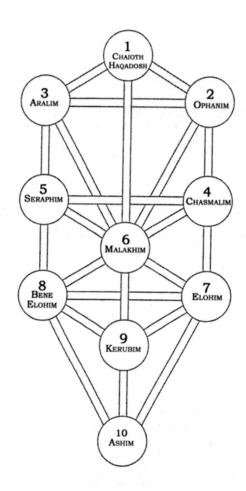

THE ORDERS OF ANGELS OF THE SEPHIROTH

Chaioth haQadosh

"Their gait is like the appearance of the lightning, their appearance is like the appearance of the rainbow in the cloud, their faces are like the appearance of the bride, their wings are like the radiance of the clouds of glory."[25]

The *Chaioth haQadosh* (*'Holy Living Creatures'*) are known as the Seraphim in the grimoires, being the *"Seraphim who being inflamed or enlightened do enlighten all"*.[26] The Chaioth haQadosh embody the perfect flame of love, and should be called when this is sought. They are considered overwhelming, and their presence may cause discomfort particularly without protection. Unlike other angelic beings which are usually considered to be made from the highest aspect of the element of Air, the Chaioth HaQadosh are seen as being fiery beings, with fiery breath.

Vision:

In appearance the Chaioth ha Qadosh have the body of a man, with four faces, of the four elemental creatures of Man (Air), Lion (Fire), Eagle (Water) and Bull (Earth). Each one has two pairs of wings, and their feet are described as being like the sole of a calf's foot, and of burnished bronze. The angels appear joined in a circle, with wings linked on either side, and with an amber-coloured fire between them, from which shoots forth lightning.

---

[25] *Hekhalot Zutarti.*

[26] Sloane MS 3825.

Ophanim

The *Ophanim* (*'Wheels'*) are known as the Kerubim in the grimoires, *"who being full of knowledge do teach"*.[27] The Ophanim should be called upon for wisdom, and to grasp extremely complex or subtle concepts, and when contemplating the divine. They may also be called when striving for illumination.

Vision:

In appearance the Ophanim are described as looking like huge wheels, of beryl colour (i.e. aquamarine), with many eyes on the rims of the wheel.

Aralim

The *Aralim* or *Eralim* (*'Strong and Mighty Ones'*) are known as the Order of Thrones in the grimoires, being described as the *"Thrones whereon God sitteth"*.[28] The Aralim should be called upon to help you make correct judgments, especially when faced with difficult choices and no obvious solutions. Further they should also be called upon when contemplating the divine and eternity.

Vision:

In appearance the Aralim stand about 2m tall, with beautiful though somewhat severe faces. They wear black tunics and gold crowns. They have white wings on their backs, and rainbows play about them at all times.

---

[27] Sloane MS 3825.
[28] Sloane MS 3825.

Chasmalim

The *Chasmalim* (*'Brilliant Ones'*) are known as the Order of Dominations in the grimoires, being those *"who do excel others"*.[29] The Chasmalim should be called upon for focusing your will, and refining your senses, as well as resisting strong temptations which are not beneficial to your development (though they may appeal to your hedonistic side). They may also be called to help overcome your enemies, internal and external.

Vision:

The Chasmalim stand about 2m tall, and are extremely beautiful, with white wings. They wear sapphire blue tunics, and give off an aura of intense light that makes it difficult to look at them.

The Seraphim

The *Seraphim* (*'Burning Ones'*, or possibly *'Fiery Serpents'*) are known as the Order of Potestates or Powers in the grimoires, being *"those who do restrain the devil"*.[30] The Seraphim should be called upon for spiritual protection from negative influences or entities (including people), and for overcoming passions or negative emotions which are detrimental to your growth.

Vision:

In appearance the Seraphim are very beautiful angels, around 2m tall with who have three pairs of white wings on their backs, in scarlet tunics, whose auras are filled with flames that surround them at all times.

---

[29] Sloane MS 3825.
[30] Sloane MS 3825.

The Malachim

The *Malachim* (*'Kings'* or *'Kingly Ones'*) are known as the Order of Virtues in the grimoires, being those *"by whom signs and miracles are wrought"*.[31] The Malachim should be called upon to strengthen the will, courage, humility and patience, and aid the caller in coping with adversity and trauma. When truth is required is also a good time to work with them.

Vision:

In appearance the Malachim stand about 2m tall, and are very beautiful. They have white wings, and wear golden tunics and have golden crowns on their heads. All around them there is an intense aura of nobility and grace.

The Elohim

The *Elohim* (*'Gods'*) are known as the Order of Principalities in the grimoires, being those *"who rule over others"*.[32] The Elohim should be called upon to improve your personal situation so you can more effectively fulfil your spiritual path, and also how to handle power so it is not abused but used positively.

Vision:

The Elohim are seen as standing about 2m tall, with white wings and are very beautiful. Some have more masculine faces and some more feminine. They wear emerald green tunics and are surrounded by an aura of beauty.

---

[31] Sloane MS 3825.

[32] Sloane MS 3825.

The Bene Elohim

The *Bene Elohim* ('*Sons of the Gods*') are known as the Order of Archangels in the grimoires, being those *"who extendeth the greater messages"*.[33] They should be called upon to strengthen the mind and intuition, increase precognition and spiritual devotion; and may be called upon when dealing with the animal kingdom.

Vision:

In appearance the Bene Elohim stand about 2m tall with white wings and are very beautiful. Some of them appear more masculine, and some more feminine. They wear orange tunics.

The Kerubim

The *Kerubim* ('*Strong Ones*') are known as the Order of Angels in the grimoires, being those *"who perform the lesser messages"*.[34] The Kerubim should be called upon for sustenance through troubles, and for guidance in dealing with immediate problems. They may also be called upon when dealing with the plant kingdom. The Kerubim are the most elemental of the Orders of Angels, and are probably the easiest to contact for this reason.

Vision:

The elemental nature of the Kerubim is seen in their appearance. They have two sets of wings, one set pointing upwards and one set downwards; and each has a head of one of the four elemental animals – eagle, lion, man and bull.

---

[33] Sloane MS 3825.

[34] Sloane Ms 3825.

The Ashim

The *Ashim* (*'Flames'*) or *Issim* are known as the Order of Blessed Souls in the grimoires. They are also known as the Animastic Order or Order of the Saints. From this perspective, if you wished to include working with the saints in your practices, this is the appropriate attribution. The Ashim should be called upon for dealing with healing, crafts and skills, and work with elemental beings. Additionally they may be called upon when dealing with the mineral kingdom.

Vision:

The Ashim appear as small dancing blue flames.

CHAPTER 11

The Heavens

The term *'Heavens'* is somewhat misleading, as in Qabalah the term is applied to the (largely) planetary attributions of the Sephiroth. This then refers to the tangible physical presence equated to the Sephiroth in the material universe, not the afterlife realms of angels and souls. From this we see how the Tree of Life is represented in our galaxy, from the initial divine manifestation of Kether (*'the big bang'*), through the stars of the zodiac (Chokmah), the seven classical planets (Binah to Yesod) and the four elements (Malkuth).

Malkuth as often described as representing planet Earth, and this is correct inasmuch as it is the tangible combination of the four elements which provides a basis on which human life exists. So it is both the Earth, and the elements which make up the earth. At the opposite end of the Tree, demonstrating the magical principle of *'As above, so below'*, is Kether. Where Malkuth represents the four elements manifest and in motion, Kether represents the four elements moving from being unmanifest towards creation.

The elemental basis of the Tree of Life is an important consideration, as it demonstrates again the way patterns occur and repeat throughout the Tree. Thus if we consider the other eight Sephiroth between Kether and Malkuth, they all have elemental attributions which connect to their planetary attributions. Indeed the four elements occur in the lower Tree, and again in the upper Tree, which can also be seen as those powers within us (the lower Tree) and in action outside us (the upper Tree).

The planetary and elemental nature of the heavens of the Sephiroth is the interface for practical Qabalistic magick for tangible results. Essentially it is the form of Assiah, the *'Making World'*, with the Heaven representing the part of each Sephira that partakes of Assiah. Any magick with a material base, such as talismanic magick or healing partakes of the nature of Assiah. The *Table of Intentions* given in the first chapter gives an indication of which Sephira is the best for working for particular results.

The Elements & the Sephiroth

Sephira	Heaven	Element
Kether	First Swirlings	All Four Elements Unmanifest
Chokmah	Zodiac	Air
Binah	Saturn	Earth
Chesed	Jupiter	Water
Geburah	Mars	Fire
Tiphereth	Sun	Fire
Netzach	Venus	Earth
Hod	Mercury	Air
Yesod	Moon	Water
Malkuth	Four Elements	All Four Elements Manifest

The word Achad (AChD) which means *unity*, is often applied to the Tree of Life, and demonstrates the nature of the heavens on the Tree. Although it adds to thirteen, it breaks down into its three component letters, which demonstrate the Tree of Life – from the Unity of Kether (Aleph = 1), through the eight planetary (and zodiacal) Sephiroth from Chokmah to Yesod (Cheth = 8) to the Elemental Sephira of Malkuth (Daleth = 4, the Four Elements).

CHAPTER 12

Magick through the Worlds

The Worlds in the Tree of Life act as a process of manifestation down the Tree and of realisation up the Tree. Both directions are valid and appropriate depending on the desired result. Prayer can combine both of the directions, as although prayers for results are directed up the Tree, their result if successful is then manifest down the Tree.

The directional effect of magick on the Tree can be seen in the parts of the soul. For manifestation, the process moves from the intangible to the tangible. This is seen through the realisation from the immeasurable soul forces known as *makifim* (envelopments) into the manifest world. The beginning of any magical manifestation is in the divine self (*Yechidah*), which formulates the intent (*Chayah*). The intent is then given its first subtle definition within the body through the process of thought (*Neshamah*). From thought the intent is formulated, named (*Ruach*) and given a precise pattern within which it may manifest. This being achieved, the appropriate set of ritual actions (*Nephesh*) are enacted, be they meditation, vibration of divine names, conjuration or whatever is deemed appropriate. Finally this results in the manifestation of the result corresponding to the physical body (*Guph*).

For the process of realisation, the opposite direction is followed. Thus something occurs which causes an initial insight, which can be considered the manifestation (*Guph*). This then leads to action (*Nephesh*) to act on the insight, including talking about it (*Ruach*) to give it a clearer form, whether in internal dialogue or to others. The next stage is to focus one's thoughts (*Neshamah*) on the expansion of the original insight through these processes. These expansions turn the insight into a realisation (*Chayah*), which if profound may lead to readjustment or realignment of the self with a greater understanding of the divine (*Yechidah*).

World	Principle	Contains	Part of Soul	Soul Impulse
Atziluth	Archetypal	Kether Chokmah Binah	Yechidah Chayah Neshamah	Divinity Intent Thought
Briah	Creative	Chesed Geburah Tiphereth	Ruach	Speech
Yetzirah	Formative	Netzach Hod Yesod	Nephesh	Action
Assiah	Making	Malkuth	Guph	Manifestation

The expression of the process may also be described in terms of the Four Worlds. The direction of the flow of energy for manifestation is from the initial creative urge in Kether (in the first World of Atziluth) to the final physical reality of Malkuth (in the fourth World of Assiah). In Atziluth pure will creates the perfect template of the initial impulse or emanation. This corresponds to the Divine Name, representing the absolute divine essence, the highest aspect of anything. From Atziluth the Archangels of Briah act as lenses, enabling the ultimate force to take form into patterns of order that enable the further manifestation of energy towards matter. The pure will and ideas of Atziluth become formed into concepts in Briah.

In the third World of Yetzirah, the Angels come into being, realising the concepts of Briah and acting as distributors of the patterns of order created by the Archangels who rule them. The worlds of Briah and Yetzirah together contain the six Sephiroth from Chesed to Yesod, which are collectively called the Sephiroth of Construction, as they combine the processes of conceptualization and realisation. In the fourth World of Assiah, matter is formed, enabling the manifestation of physicality. This is why Assiah is also called the Universe of Forms.

World	Atziluth	Briah	Yetzirah	Assiah
Action	Emanating	Creating	Forming	Making
Process	Intent	Concept	Realisation	Manifestation
Divinity	Divine Name	Archangel	Order of Angels	Heaven
Tetragrammaton	Yod	Heh	Vav	Heh (final)
Element	Fire	Water	Air	Earth

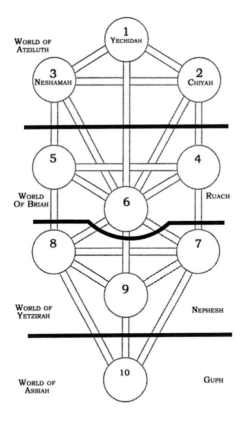

THE FOUR WORLDS AND THE PARTS OF THE SOUL

CHAPTER 13

Talismanic Magick

There is a long tradition of amulets and talismans being used in Qabalistic magick. Amulets are used for protection, and were frequently made using verses from the Psalms on pieces of parchment, which were placed in boxes and tied to the arms (or head), and called *Tefillim* (*phylacteries*). Talismans are used for attraction, and may be made on paper, or using the appropriate planetary metals.

Construction of Talismans

Talismans are not made in isolation. Rather the process requires preparation, and the following steps should be followed:

- Determine the appropriate Sephira, and then work out the appropriate day and hours for creating the talisman (see Appendix 4 - Planetary Timings). You should also check against the table of suitable days to ensure you have the optimum timing.
- Decide on the shape of the talisman. This will most often be on paper (or parchment or card), and so may be drawn in appropriate colour ink. A white background is the standard. A circle is a good shape for a talisman, or you can also opt for a shape with a number of sides equal to the number of the Sephira (from 3 for Binah, to 10 for Malkuth).

- Decide on the word components of the talisman. This is often done in the shape of circles, hexagrams, and magick squares.

Sephira	Divine Name	Planet	Colour	Metal	Crystals
Kether	Eheieh	First Swirlings	White	White Gold	Diamond, Zircon
Chokmah	Yah	Zodiac	Grey	Platinum	Labradorite, Star Sapphire
Binah	Yahveh	Saturn	Black	Lead	Jet, Obsidian, Smoky Quartz, Star Ruby
Chesed	El	Jupiter	Blue	Tin	Lapis Lazuli, Sapphire, Sodalite, Turquoise
Geburah	Elohim Givor	Mars	Red	Iron	Bloodstone, Garnet, Magnetite, Ruby
Tiphereth	Eloah	Sun	Gold	Gold	Amber, Sunstone, Topaz
Netzach	Yahveh Zavaot	Venus	Green	Copper	Emerald, Jade, Malachite, Rose Quartz
Hod	Elohim Zavaot	Mercury	Orange	Aluminium	Agate, Citrine Quartz, Opal
Yesod	Shaddai	Moon	Silver	Silver	Chalcedony, Moonstone, Pearl, Quartz
Malkuth	Adonai Melekh	Elements	Brown	Bronze	Aventurine, Chrysocolla, Marble, Onyx

In *The Book of the Signs of the Zodiac*, in *Sepher Raziel*, is an intriguing list of appropriate and inappropriate days for creating amulets and talismans. We have included this information here in the following table, to provide a further refinement for the timing of talismanic construction. The use of positive and negative days goes back to ancient Egypt, and continued into the grimoire tradition (e.g. the *Hygromantia*) as well as Qabalistic works (e.g. Sepher Raziel). Note the list only gives thirty days in the month, so the suitability of the thirty-first day is a matter for your choice. Clearly this list needs to be combined with the days of the week and planetary hours to find optimum timings.

Day of the Month	Suitability	Day of the Month	Suitability
First	Anytime	Sixteenth	Morning
Second	Morning	Seventeenth	Evening
Third	Not	Eighteenth	Not
Fourth	Anytime	Nineteenth	Not
Fifth	Morning	Twentieth	Not
Sixth	Not	Twenty-first	Morning
Seventh	Morning	Twenty-second	Anytime
Eighth	Morning	Twenty-third	Not
Ninth	Not	Twenty-fourth	Morning
Tenth	Not	Twenty-fifth	Anytime
Eleventh	Morning	Twenty-sixth	Not
Twelfth	Anytime	Twenty-seventh	Morning
Thirteenth	Not	Twenty-eighth	Anytime
Fourteenth	Morning	Twenty-ninth	Not
Fifteenth	Not	Thirtieth	Morning

Consecration of Talismans

There seems to be a great deal of confusion about the consecration of talismans. Many works describe a purificatory practice and call it consecration. However consecration is a process of sanctification and dedication to a specific purpose. This is achieved through the directed intent of the practitioner, and may be performed following a purification of the talisman so it is ready for consecration.

When you have made your talisman you need to purify and consecrate it. You will need the following ingredients:

- The talisman.

- An appropriately coloured piece of silk big enough to wrap it in.
- A bowl of salt
- A bowl of water
- Some incense or joss
- Almond oil

Purification:

Having worked out the time for your ritual beforehand, and created your talisman, place it on a piece of appropriately coloured silk. And hold this at chest height in front of you.

Vibrate the Divine Name of the associated Sephira, and as you exhale, see the energy you project with your intent, charged with the Divine Name, form into a sphere of luminous energy (of the appropriate colour for the Sephira and Divine Name) about 20cm in diameter in the air around the talisman.

State the intent of the talisman, in a single concise sentence (that you have prepared beforehand).

Pass the talisman through the incense or joss the appropriate (to the planet) number of times, as you do saying:

> *I purify this talisman with the emanating power of Fire that it may (repeat intent).*
> *Sprinkle the talisman with water, as you do saying,*
> *I purify this talisman with the creative power of Water that it may (repeat intent).*
> *Breathe upon the talisman the appropriate (to the planet) number of times, as you do saying:*
> *I purify this talisman with the formative power of Air that it may (repeat intent).*
> *Sprinkle the talisman with salt, as you do saying*
> *I purify this talisman with the active power of Earth that it may (repeat intent).*
> *Anoint the talisman with a drop of almond oil, saying:*

I purify this talisman with the power of the divine name Yahveh that it may (repeat intent).

(Note Yahveh should be intoned using the vibratory formula).

- See the sphere shrink, becoming brighter, and being absorbed into the talisman.

Consecration:

Perform the Lightning Flash affirmation, but at the end instead of putting your hands over your heart, place them on the talisman and see the energy you have drawn down through the entire Tree of Life in yourself passing into the talisman to empower it, saying:

> *I will take of my spirit and put it upon this;*
> *I have created this for my glory,*
> *I have formed it,*
> *Yea, I have made it.*

Wrap the talisman in the silk and put it in a safe place.

(The words you speak are adapted reflections of the Biblical verses which are said to be the origins of the names of the Four Worlds. These are *Numbers 11:17, "And I will take [Atziluth] of the spirit which is upon these, and will put it upon them"*; and *Isaiah 43:7, "I have created [Briah] him for my glory, I have formed [Yetzirah] him; yea, I have made [Assiah] him."*)

You can of course use discs of metals or crystals for making amulets and talismans. Whilst some of these would be prohibitively expensive (such as gold), it is an option.

CHAPTER 14

Polarity Work

The Sephiroth of the Tree of Life all lie vertically within three columns, known as Pillars. These three pillars represent many concepts and symbols, most of which revolve around the idea of a harmony between two opposing forces. The three pillars are sometimes referred to as the *zahzahoth* (hidden splendours), a term used to denote the underlying balance of opposing forces of primordial mercy and primordial justice by primordial will.

The Black and White Pillars are hinted at in *I Kings 7:14*, where the artisan Hiram is described as *"Filled with wisdom and understanding and skill"*. As the Temple itself corresponds to the Tree of Life, it can be seen that Hiram is being likewise compared with the two outer pillars, by being filled with wisdom (Chokmah) and understanding (Binah), the capitals of those two Pillars. Furthermore, the balance of wisdom and understanding, or the two outer pillars, is skill, their balance in the middle pillar.

When we consider the Four Worlds, we can see that all three of the Pillars exist in the upper three Worlds of Atziluth, Briah and Yetzirah, but only the Middle Pillar, of balance, exists in the material World of Assiah. This is significant, as it emphasises the fact that to achieve successful transformation you always need to have equilibrium and balance to achieve a tangible result.

Meditation on the Scales of Balance

Verse 2:1 of the *Sepher Yetzirah* introduces an important concept for working with the polarity of the pillars to transform the self, with the three Mother letters of the Hebrew alphabet being equated to the three Pillars. It states:

> *"The Three Mothers are Aleph Mem Shin, their foundation is a pan of merit, a pan of liability, and the tongue of decree deciding between them. Mem hums, Shin hisses, and Aleph is the Breath of air deciding between them"*

Mem represents the pan of merit, Shin the pan of liability, and Aleph the fulcrum and pointer (tongue of decree) in the centre. To contextualize the meditation, it is necessary to consider the meaning of two of the words in this verse. The word used here for *'pan'* is *Kaph*, which is also the palm of the hand. The word for *'tongue'* is *Lashon*, which is normally used for the tongue in the mouth. From these meanings comes the key to the technique for this meditation.

Facing East, stand straight with your arms outstretched and straight to the sides, so you make a cross. Your left hand represents the pan of merit and your right the pan of liability, your body is the fulcrum. See yourself as the scales of balance made by these letters.

If you wish to improve the a good quality in yourself (merit) or a situation, hum Mem as a mantra (*"Mem hums"*) for several minutes whilst seeing the letter Mem in white (symbolising the White Pillar) in your left hand. Slowly move your left arm down, and your right arm correspondingly up, to show the balance tipping in favour of the merit. Do this slowly to an angle of up to 30°.

If you wish to redress a mistake or bad behaviour you have made (liability), hiss Shin as a mantra (*"Shin hisses"*) for several minutes whilst seeing the letter Shin in black (symbolising the Black Pillar) in your right hand. Slowly move your right arm down and your left arm correspondingly up to an angle of up to 30° to show your acknowledgement of your mistake. Then change this pattern by just concentrating on your breathing (*"Aleph is the Breath of air deciding between them"*). Then return to humming Mem as a mantra for several minutes, slowly moving your arms back to the horizontal, showing your intent to transform the mistake or behaviour.

These meditations can be performed once or repeated as often as you feel necessary to achieve the desired effect. The initial posture for both meditations is facing East, standing straight with your arms outstretched horizontally forming a cross.

Pillar of Severity	Pillar of Harmony	Pillar of Mercy
Primordial Justice	Primordial Will	Primordial Mercy
Judgement	Balance	Love
Black	Grey	White
Negative	Neutral	Positive
Passive	Stillness	Active
Feminine	Androgyne	Masculine
Form	Transition	Force
Matter	Spirit	Energy
Fire	White Light or Air	Water
Shin	Aleph	Mem
Restraint/Constriction	Equilibrium	Expansion
Binah, Geburah, Hod	Kether, Tiphereth, Yesod, Malkuth	Chokmah, Chesed, Netzach

CHAPTER 15

Temples of the Sephiroth

The temples of the Sephiroth are astral locations produced with their appropriate energy, within which you focus entirely on the energy of the specific Sephira. By concentrating the appropriate symbols and energies together, you effectively create a magnet which draws in more of the type of energy you desire, and also provides an interface for you and the beings of the Sephira. When you create a Sephirotic temple you are moulding malleable energies into a suitable form, which is fixed by your will with your intent. It is important that you are very precise and consistent with the details you include, to ensure the increased effectiveness of the temple over time for your workings.

Unlike the temples visited in pathworkings, these temples can be used in any sequence. Whereas pathworkings generally start from the Malkuth temple and work up the Tree, the Sephirotic temples are visited directly, so e.g. if you wanted to work in the Geburah temple, you go straight there rather than through a sequence of other temples. These temples are spaces for active magical acts, not the passive self-exploration of pathworking. As a result, you may encounter the beings of the Sephiroth, such as the ruling archangel and angels from the appropriate order, within the temple, even when you have not specifically invited them. If this is the case, do not hesitate to ask for their aid in making your magick work more effectively and speedily.

The following details are standard to all the temples. They are all circular, their shape matching that of the classic magick circle. They are

15m in diameter and have walls which extend up 3m from the floor to a domed ceiling. In the north of the temple are two pillars, of 1m diameter each, 2m apart, rising 3m from the floor towards the ceiling, these pillars are 1m in from the wall. The left pillar is black and made of onyx, the right pillar is white and made of marble. Both pillars are capped with a carved crown, representing the supernal Sephiroth of Chokmah (white) and Binah (black).

Remember that when you work in a temple, you can see whatever you choose there as magical tools. E.g. you may see a mirror or crystal for having visions, or wield a sword. Likewise how you see yourself dressed is relevant, with regard to appropriate colours, and magical jewellery. Of course you may choose to mirror what you are wearing in the physical world, which then helps provide a link between the subtle and the tangible. Remember though that in such cases, everything on your person should have been consecrated beforehand (even down to glasses or contact lenses!).

Malkuth Temple

The best-known Qabalistic temple image must be that of the Malkuth temple, with its black and white pillars, double-cube altar and black and white checked floor. The floor resembles a chessboard, and reminds us that life can indeed be considered a game, where the rules are not fixed and people play either as pawns or higher pieces. Making a conscious decision to follow a spiritual path such as the Qabalah and develop yourself is a signal to the universe that you are not simply a pawn to the whim of others, but rather a more active force seeking to evolve and create positive change.

Vision:

The Malkuth temple is circular with white marble walls, with delicate yellow, red, blue and black veins. The domed hemi-spherical ceiling is made of lapis lazuli, deep azure blue flecked with gold. The floor of the temple is made of onyx and marble squares, 1m square like a chessboard. In the centre of the temple, set on top of the meeting of four squares, stands a white marble double-cube altar, 1m in height and 0.5m square on the top. On the top of the altar is a small bronze bowl, in which burns an undying blue flame, the flame of spirit. In the north are two pillars, of 1m diameter each, 2m apart, rising from the floor to the ceiling, these pillars are 1m in from the wall. The left pillar is black and made of onyx, the right pillar is white and made of marble. Hanging in the air 2m off the ground between the pillars you see the divine name Adonai Melekh (ADNI MLK) in letters of brown flame. You stand beneath the letters and vibrate the name, and as you do so the letters all turn into a wave of brown light which flows over you and is absorbed into your body.

Yesod Temple

"When I ascended to the first palace, I was righteous."[35]

The Yesod temple is unique amongst the temples in that it has an element of flux in its appearance. The Yesod temple never remains exactly the same, expressing its lunar nature, and the patterns on the walls reflect this.

Vision:

The Yesod temple is circular, with walls made from a swirling pattern of grey and purple semi-solid mist. The domed hemi-spherical ceiling is made of lapis lazuli, deep azure blue flecked with gold. The floor of the temple is made of made of marble, with a 9-rayed star in amethyst-purple spanning the whole floor. In the centre of the temple there is a white marble double-cube altar, 1m in height and 0.5m square on the top. On the top of the altar is a small silver bowl, in which burns an undying blue flame, the flame of spirit.

In the north are two pillars, of 1m diameter each, 2m apart, rising from the floor to the ceiling, these pillars are 1m in from the wall. The left pillar is black and made of onyx, the right pillar is white and made of marble. Hanging in the air 2m off the ground between the pillars you see the divine name Shaddai (ShDI) in letters of silver flame. You stand beneath the letters and vibrate the name, and as you do so the letters all turn into a wave of silver light which flows over you and is absorbed into your body.

---

[35] *Maaseh Merkavah*, 558.

Hod Temple

"In the second palace I was pure."[36]

The Hod temple partakes of the quicksilver essence of Mercury, hard to pin down and keep to a clear and precise form. Hod can be distracting, and it is important to keep your awareness focused when in this temple.

Vision:

The Hod temple is circular, with walls made from opal, white with flashes of red, blue, yellow and green which catch the eye as you move around. The domed hemi-spherical ceiling is made of lapis lazuli, deep azure blue flecked with gold. The floor of the temple is made of Citrine quartz, inlaid with an 8-rayed silver star whose tips reach the walls. In the centre of the temple there is a marble double-cube altar, 1m in height and 0.5m square on the top. On the top of the altar is a small silver bowl, in which burns an undying blue flame, the flame of spirit.

In the north are two pillars, of 1m diameter each, 2m apart, rising from the floor to the ceiling, these pillars are 1m in from the wall. The left pillar is black and made of onyx, the right pillar is white and made of marble. Hanging in the air 2m off the ground between the pillars you see the divine name Elohim Zavaot (ALHIM TzBAVTh) in letters of orange flame. You stand beneath the letters and vibrate the name, and as you do so the letters all turn into a wave of orange light which flows over you and is absorbed into your body.

---

[36] *Maaseh Merkavah*, 558.

Netzach Temple

"In the third palace, I was truthful."[37]

The Netzach temple is a place for contemplating the nature of eternity and victory. Here you will be assuming the mantle of love, and powering your intent with the emotional depths of your being, the emotional strength which needs to be tempered through regular use, like a sword.

Vision:

The Netzach temple is circular, with walls made of white marble shot through with misty veins of green. The domed hemi-spherical ceiling is made of lapis lazuli, deep azure blue flecked with gold. The floor of the temple is made of rose quartz, with a 7-rayed star in green malachite spanning the whole floor. Within the centre of the seven-pointed star is a red 7-petalled rose. In the centre of the temple there is a marble double-cube altar, 1m in height and 0.5m square on the top. On the top of the altar is a small copper bowl, in which burns an undying blue flame, the flame of spirit.

In the north are two pillars, of 1m diameter each, 2m apart, rising from the floor to the ceiling, these pillars are 1m in from the wall. The left pillar is black and made of onyx, the right pillar is white and made of marble. Hanging in the air 2m off the ground between the pillars you see the divine name Jahveh Zavaot (IHVH TzBAVTh) in letters of green flame. You stand beneath the letters and vibrate the name, and as you do so the letters all turn into a wave of green light which flows over you and is absorbed into your body.

---

[37] *Maaseh Merkavah*, 558.

Tiphereth Temple

"In the fourth palace, I was perfect."[38]

The Tiphereth temple is the heart of the Tree of Life, as the Sun is the heart of our solar system. This is the place of balance in the middle of the Tree, to which you should always return. If you are ever unsure of which temple to use, Tiphereth is always a good choice.

Vision:

The Tiphereth temple is circular, with walls made from tiger's eye, with veins of amber, brown and black shades running through them. The domed hemi-spherical ceiling is made of lapis lazuli, deep azure blue flecked with gold. The floor of the temple is made of sunstone, inlaid with a gold hexagram whose tips reach the walls. Within the centre of the hexagram is a golden sun design, with six larger rays reaching out to touch the points of the inner hexagon. In the centre of the temple standing on the centre of the sun design there is a marble double-cube altar, 1m in height and 0.5m square on the top. On the top of the altar is a small gold bowl, in which burns an undying blue flame, the flame of spirit.

In the north are two pillars, of 1m diameter each, 2m apart, rising from the floor to the ceiling, these pillars are 1m in from the wall. The left pillar is black and made of onyx, the right pillar is white and made of marble. Hanging in the air 2m off the ground between the pillars you see the divine name Eloah (ALVH) in letters of gold flame. You stand beneath the letters and vibrate the name, and as you do so the letters all turn into a wave of gold light which flows over you and is absorbed into your body.

---

[38] *Maaseh Merkavah*, 558.

Geburah Temple

"In the fifth palace, I brought holiness before the king of Kings, blessed be His name."[39]

This temple is a good place for making difficult decisions, where you need to assert yourself and cut off from any external influences. The power and invisibility combination of Geburah makes it an ideal place for considering options.

Vision:

The Geburah temple is circular, with walls made of garnet. The domed hemi-spherical ceiling is made of lapis lazuli, deep azure blue flecked with gold. The floor of the temple is made of marble, inlaid with an iron pentagram whose tips reach the walls. In the centre of the temple there is a marble double-cube altar, 1m in height and 0.5m square on the top. On the top of the altar is a small iron bowl, in which burns an undying blue flame, the flame of spirit.

In the north are two pillars, of 1m diameter each, 2m apart, rising from the floor to the ceiling, these pillars are 1m in from the wall. The left pillar is black and made of onyx, the right pillar is white and made of marble. Hanging in the air 2m off the ground between the pillars you see the divine name Elohim Givor (ALHIM GBVR) in letters of scarlet red flame. You stand beneath the letters and vibrate the name, and as you do so the letters all turn into a wave of scarlet red light which flows over you and is absorbed into your body.

---

[39] *Maaseh Merkavah*, 558.

Chesed Temple

> *"In the sixth palace, I said the sanctification before Him who spoke and fashioned and commanded all living beings, so that the angel would not destroy me."*[40]

This temple is the last of them below the Veil of the Abyss, and as such it is a place of holiness, for purification and preparation for major works. It is also the place to work when you wish to develop your fortunes.

Vision:

The Chesed temple is circular, with walls made of blood red marble with white speckles. The domed hemi-spherical ceiling is made of lapis lazuli, deep azure blue flecked with gold, as is the floor. In the centre of the temple there is a marble double-cube altar, 1m in height and 0.5m square on the top. On the top of the altar is a small tin bowl, in which burns an undying blue flame, the flame of spirit.

In the north are two pillars, of 1m diameter each, 2m apart, rising from the floor to the ceiling, these pillars are 1m in from the wall. The left pillar is black and made of onyx, the right pillar is white and made of marble. Hanging in the air 2m off the ground between the pillars you see the divine name El (AL) in letters of blue flame. You stand beneath the letters and vibrate the name, and as you do so the letters all turn into a wave of blue light which flows over you and is absorbed into your body.

---

[40] *Maaseh Merkavah*, 558.

Binah Temple

"In the seventh palace, I stood in all my power. I trembled in all my limbs."[41]

This temple is somewhat sombre by nature, being aligned with the force-form interface of Binah. There is a sense of the duality of life and death in this temple, which gives a feeling of balance and equilibrium here, which can be very valuable.

Vision:

The Binah temple is circular, with walls made of shiny black obsidian, as is the floor. The domed hemi-spherical ceiling is made of lapis lazuli, deep azure blue flecked with gold. In the centre of the temple there is a marble double-cube altar, 1m in height and 0.5m square on the top. On the top of the altar is a small lead bowl, in which burns an undying blue flame, the flame of spirit.

In the north are two pillars, of 1m diameter each, 2m apart, rising from the floor to the ceiling, these pillars are 1m in from the wall. The left pillar is black and made of onyx, the right pillar is white and made of marble. Hanging in the air 2m off the ground between the pillars you see the divine name Yahveh (IHVH) in letters of black flame. You stand beneath the letters and vibrate the name, and as you do so the letters all turn into a wave of black light which flows over you and is absorbed into your body.

---

[41] *Maaseh Merkavah*, 558.

Chokmah Temple

"I am a child of earth and starry heaven, but my race is of heaven alone."[42]

The Chokmah temple could equally be known as the Temple of the Stars. It is a place of opening up your horizons and accepting that only you can make the choices you need. Chokmah is also a place to recharge your spiritual batteries when you feel disconnected or dryness.

Vision:

The Chokmah temple is circular, with walls made of labradorite, grey shot through with flashes of blue and occasional flashes of yellow, red and green. The floor is made of white marble. The ceiling is open, revealing the night sky above you. In the centre of the temple there is a marble double-cube altar, 1m in height and 0.5m square on the top. On the top of the altar is a small platinum bowl, in which burns an undying blue flame, the flame of spirit.

In the north are two pillars, of 1m diameter each, 2m apart, rising from the floor to the ceiling, these pillars are 1m in from the wall. The left pillar is black and made of onyx, the right pillar is white and made of marble. Hanging in the air 2m off the ground between the pillars you see the divine name Yah (IH) in letters of grey flame. You stand beneath the letters and vibrate the name, and as you do so the letters all turn into a wave of grey light which flows over you and is absorbed into your body.

---

[42] Orphic Oath.

Kether Temple

"When colour goes home into the eyes,
And lights that shine are shut again
With dancing girls and sweet birds' cries
Behind the gateways of the brain;
And that no-place which gave them birth, shall close
The rainbow and the rose."[43]

The temple of Kether can be very obscure, with unexpected images or symbols sometimes appearing. This is because it is your place of connection to the divine, and the divine has a sometimes annoying habit of being cryptic.

Vision:

The Kether temple is circular, with the walls and floors made of marble. The domed hemi-spherical ceiling is made of lapis lazuli, deep azure blue flecked with gold. In the centre of the temple there is a marble double-cube altar, 1m in height and 0.5m square on the top. On the top of the altar is a small white gold bowl, in which burns an undying blue flame, the flame of spirit.

In the south are two pillars, of 1m diameter each, 2m apart, rising from the floor to the ceiling, these pillars are 1m in from the wall. The left pillar is black and made of onyx, the right pillar is white and made of marble. Hanging in the air 2m off the ground between the pillars you see the divine name Eheieh (AHIH) in letters of brilliant white flame. You stand beneath the letters and vibrate the name, and as you do so the letters all turn into a wave of brilliant white light which flows over you and is absorbed into your body.

---

[43] *The Treasure*, Rupert Brooke (1887-1915).

Looking around you see a lamp in the apex of the dome, emanating a brilliant light which fills the whole temple, bathing everything in a radiance which makes it seem holy and pure.

CHAPTER 16

The Lightning Flash Exercise

The Lightning Flash is a name given to the path of creation through the Sephiroth of the Tree of Life. It is the quickest route from Kether down to Malkuth, taken by the energy as the emanation of energy in each Sephira overflowed and rushed into the next Sephira below. The Lightning Flash does not follow all the paths of the Tree of Life, as it represents the fastest route from top to bottom which passes through all the Sephiroth in turn, not the complete Tree It is also known as the Flaming Sword, as described in *Genesis 3:24*, where it says:

> "So He drove out the man; and He placed at the east of the garden of Eden the Kerubim, and the flaming sword which turned every way, to keep the way to the tree of life."

In keeping with the nature of the Lightning Flash, the exercise follows the same path of creation through your body, ensuring all your energy centres are activated and balanced ready for any subsequent work.

The Lightning Flash exercise is designed to balance out your energies, whilst at the same time connecting you to those energies in the world around you. Thus it is a process of expressing *'As Above, so below'*, by consciously identifying yourself with the Tree of Life. This exercise may be used as a precursor to any other work.

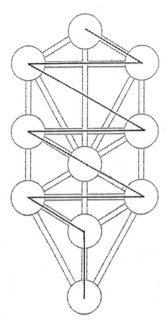

THE LIGHTNING FLASH

Lightning Flash Exercise

Above your head see a sphere of brilliant (white) light about 30cm in diameter, almost touching the top of your head. When you can feel the energy of the brilliant sphere clearly, see the energy descending as a line of white light like a flash of lightning, and as it touches the top of your head vibrate the divine name AHIH (*Ee-hay-ya*), seeing the air you inhale as brilliant white.

See the white lightning flash descend to the left side of your face, activating a 20cm sphere of pure grey light, which touches your left cheek. As this occurs, vibrate the divine name IH (*Yah*) seeing the air you inhale as pure grey.

See the lightning flash shoot horizontally through your mouth to the right side of your face, activating a 20cm sphere of black light, which is touching your right cheek at the same level as the previous sphere. As this occurs, vibrate the divine name IHVH (*Yah-veh*) seeing the air you inhale as black.

See the lightning flash pass diagonally left through your throat. At your throat see a 20cm sphere size form, this time of brilliant lavender energy, enclosing your entire throat. As this occurs vibrate the divine name RVCh hQDSh (*Roo-ach ha Ka-dosh*) seeing the air you inhale as brilliant lavender.

See the lightning flash continue from your throat to your left shoulder, where you see a 20cm sphere of deep blue light form. As this occurs, vibrate the divine name AL (*Al*) seeing the air you inhale as deep blue.

See the lightning flash shoot horizontally across your shoulders to your right shoulder, where you see a 20cm sphere of scarlet red light form. As this occurs, vibrate the divine name ALHIM GIBVR (*El-o-heem Gi-voor*) seeing the air you inhale as scarlet red.

See the lightning flash pass diagonally down through your heart towards the left hip. At your heart, see a sphere of the same size form, of gold, enclosing your heart. As this occurs, vibrate the divine name Eloah (*El-o-ah*) seeing the air you inhale as gold.

See the lightning flash reach your lift hip, where you see a 20cm sphere of emerald green light form. As this occurs, vibrate the divine name YHVH TzBAOTh (*Yah-veh Za-va-ot*) seeing the air you inhale as emerald green.

See the lightning flash horizontally across your body to your right hip, where you see a 20cm sphere of orange light form. As this occurs, vibrate the divine name ALHIM TzBAOTh (*El-o-heem Za-va-ot*) seeing the air you inhale as orange.

See the lightning flash diagonally to the left to the region of your genitals. See a sphere of the same size form here, of silver, enclosing this region. As this occurs, vibrate the divine name ShDI (*Sha-dai*) seeing the air you inhale as silver in colour.

Finally see the lightning flash continue vertically down your legs to the soles of your feet, where it forms a similar size sphere upon which the feet stand, bright brown in colour. As this occurs, vibrate the divine name ADNI MLK (*Ah-don-ai Me-lek*) seeing the air you inhale as bright brown.

When you have done this, feel the Tree of Life within yourself. Feel all the parts of your body connected by the Lightning Flash, from your crown to the left side of your face, across to the right side, diagonally down to the throat and then to the left shoulder. From the left shoulder it continues horizontally across to the right shoulder, then diagonally down through your heart to your left hip, then horizontally across to your right hip. From your right hip it travels diagonally down to your genitals, and then vertically down your legs to your feet.

Now raise your hands to the heavens with the palms upwards and spread your fingers out, so that your arms form a 'V' shape. This is the position of the Priestly Blessing, with the ten fingers corresponding to the Sephiroth. Feel the energy of the heavens in your hands for a few seconds. Then move your hands over your heart, with your dominant hand on your heart, and the other hand over the top of it. Take a couple of deep breaths and then relax.

CHAPTER 17

Qabalah in Daily Life

As well as performing the exercises and rituals in this book, and discovering their benefits, you may wish to apply more Qabalistic principles to your daily life. By looking at any areas where you have problems, e.g. in your studies, in relationships, or in the workplace, you can see which part of your life needs to be concentrated on. By using the appropriate symbols, colours and techniques for the associated Sephira, you can focus the positive energies of that Sephira, and draw more in, creating a magnetic effect, which will then saturate your life with the energies of change, ensuring that the required transformations occur.

We are by nature creatures of habit, and one of our greatest hurdles can our resistance to change. One of the great beauties of the Qabalah is that it provides us with a map for balanced and effective change. By doing this you will bring a greater sense of balance into your life, enabling you to progress more efficiently on your path through life. By harmonising intellect and emotions, will and imagination, drive and direction, practicing Qabalah brings insight, calm and success into your life.

If you have a tendency towards obsessive behaviour, you should watch yourself carefully, as the Qabalah and the fascinating new worldviews it provides can become all consuming. It must not be allowed to completely overtake and rule your life.

Bathing

The initial references to water in the first verses of *Genesis* give an indication of the importance of water in the Qabalah. In *Genesis 1:8* we read, *"God made the sky, and it separated the water below the sky from the water above the sky. And it was so. God named the sky heaven (shamayim)."* Even the word for heaven found in this verse, *shamayim*, contains the word for water (*mayim*). The implication of this is that water is a medium of the divine, which is seen in the magical significance of dew (associated with Kether), rivers and other flowing waters. By descending from above (*'above the sky'*), through rain and dew, and returning to the heavens through evaporation (from *'below the sky'*), water embodies the principle of *'As above, so below.'*

Such water is known as *'Living Water'*, i.e. pure water which has fallen as rain or is otherwise from a natural source such as a spring, without being drawn from its source by an artificial conduit or by a human hand. Living water is found in lakes, ponds, rivers and springs, and this is why Grimoires like the *Key of Solomon* instructed the magician to bathe in a river or similar source of living water. It is also used for purifying ritual items, including talismans.

That a Qabalist must bathe before practice is clearly illustrated in *Numbers 19:17-19*, where the required purification for entering the sanctuary is described:

> *"For the man who is unclean must....bathe himself in water, and by evening he will be clean. If an unclean man fails to purify himself in this way, he must be cut off from the community for he will defile the sanctuary of the Eternal"*

Cleanliness is considered extremely important in magick, and you should bathe or shower regularly (preferably daily). Remember you can add essential oils or herbs that you feel are appropriate to your bath, and also meditate on purity and cleanliness when you are in the bath.

Diet

If you are practicing Qabalah there are certain foods you may choose to omit from your diet. These are the foodstuffs that Qabalists chose not to eat for various reasons. Traditionally pork and seafood would never be eaten. Although there are many references in the *Tanakh* to eating meat, some people go further and point to *Ezekiel 4:14*, which might suggest a vegetarian diet is preferable:

> *"Then said I, Ah Lord God! Behold, my soul hath not been polluted; for from my youth up, even till now, have I not eaten of that which dieth of itself, or is torn in pieces; neither came there abominable flesh into my mouth."*

Of course abstaining completely from animal products does tend to help increase psychic sensitivity, so there are benefits to such a course of action. Bread is usually included, though traditionally unleavened, and you should check if you have wheat or gluten allergies. Practicing Qabalah does not mean you cannot drink alcohol, but moderation is encouraged.

Using psychoactive drugs in combination with Qabalistic practice is not encouraged or recommended. Whilst some books will give you lists of drugs relating to the Sephiroth and paths, the use of these substances can result in all sorts of problems and they are not conducive to the discipline of serious magical work.

Scents

The different Sephiroth are all associated with different areas of life, and each has associated scents. You may wish to burn different scents or wear oils or perfumes for their qualities based on this. You can choose scents for different occasions to help stimulate your body and mind with the appropriate energy of the Sephira you are working with. Likewise such scents could be added to the bath to affect your mood.

So for day-to-day activities and earthy things like gardening choose Malkuthian scents, for dreams choose Yesodic scents, for study and intellectual stimulation Hod scents, for love and the emotions Netzach scents. For success you could use Tiphereth scents, for exercise Geburah scents, for health Chesedic scents. For understanding Binah scents, for wisdom and insight Chokmah scents, and for meditation and prayer Kether scents.

Sephirotic Days

You can follow the sequence of the planetary energies through the week and incorporate appropriate correspondences to help you learn them. Wear an item of clothing of the appropriate colour for the Sephira, and if possible an item of jewellery with an appropriate crystal in. Try also wearing an oil appropriate to the Sephira, on your wrists or if you feel appropriate on the part of the body corresponding to the Sephira. Watch your behaviour during the day and try to make sure you practice the virtues and avoid the vices of the Sephira. This will help you learn Qabalah in a very practical way!

Day of the Week	Planet	Sephira
Sunday	Sun	Tiphereth
Monday	Moon	Yesod
Tuesday	Mars	Geburah
Wednesday	Mercury	Hod
Thursday	Jupiter	Chesed
Friday	Venus	Netzach
Saturday	Saturn	Binah, Malkuth

CHAPTER 18

The 231 Gates

"Twenty-two Foundation Letters:
He placed them in a circle like a wall with 231 Gates.
The Circle oscillates back and forth.
A sign for this is:
There is nothing in good higher than Delight
There is nothing evil lower than Plague.
How?
He permuted them, weighed them, and transformed them,
Aleph with them all and all of them with Aleph, Beth with them all and
all of them with Beth.
They repeat in a cycle and exist in 231 Gates.
It comes out that all that is formed and all that is spoken emanates
from one Name"[44]

This verse of the *Sepher Yetzirah* describes a technique for using the Hebrew alphabet as a powerful tool for attracting or banishing things in your life. Decoding the phrases, it quickly becomes clear that the technique is to place all the letters of the Hebrew alphabet in a circle (*"He placed them in a circle Like a wall with 231 Gates."*), and connect every letter to every other letter (*"Aleph with them all and all of them with Aleph, Beth with them all and all of them with Beth."*) with a line. When every letter is joined to every other letter, you get 231 lines ($\Sigma 1\text{-}21$), which represent the 231 Gates.

---

[44] *Sepher Yetzirah* 2:4-5.

231 GATES – START

231 GATES - COMPLETE

Attracting with the 231 Gates

Sit down facing east, with the glyph in front of you. See each of the letters in turn flaming gold, starting with Aleph and working through the alphabet to Tav.

When all the letters are visible as gold fire, see a golden thread of light join from Aleph to Beth, and vibrate the combination of letters AB. Then do the same for Aleph and Gimel, seeing the gold thread and vibrating AG. Do this for Aleph with every letter, forming 21 threads of gold from Aleph to around the circle. The same procedure should then be repeated for Beth, beginning with Beth Gimel (BG), all the way to Beth Tav (BTh).

Combinations which have already been used are not repeated, so you would not vibrate Beth Aleph (BA), as you have already vibrated Aleph Beth (AB), which is the same connection. This results in less combinations for each letter going round, with Shin only being linked to Tav as Shin Tav (ShT), as all the rest of the combinations have already been performed.

At the end of this process you see a golden web of 231 strands, representing the permutations of letters that form creation. From here you can see your desired intent, and set it in the centre of the circle, amidst all the threads, powered by the energy you have raised through your intent and chanting. This is what is meant by *"There is nothing in good higher than Delight"*. See the energy gathering in the centre, and then shoot the intent upwards into the heavens to realisation.

Banishing with the 231 Gates

If you need to get rid of something, you can apply the same technique, but in reverse. Then you are working with the principle that *"There is nothing evil lower than Plague"*, where you banish an undesired influence. Thus the delight (*Oneg*, ONG) achieved through positive action is reversed by switching the sequence, producing plague (*Nega*, NGO).

To begin, you once again sit facing the glyph, facing north. This time though, see the golden fiery letters rising from the ground at the circumference starting with Tav, just to the left of North, and work anticlockwise around the circle, all the way back to Aleph in the North.

When you have done this, again create the golden threads, but start with the last combination, i.e. Tav Shin (ThSh) and chant this as you see the golden thread form, then Tav Resh (ThR), all the way to Tav Aleph (ThA). Then do the same for Shin, working anticlockwise around the circle, starting with Shin Resh (ShR) and all the way back to Shin Aleph (ShA). Repeat this for each letter until you have finished with Beth Aleph (BA). As with Attracting, you do not repeat letter combinations.

Then see the thing you wish to banish in the centre of the web of golden threads, and see it sinking into the earth, to be absorbed by the universe and taken away from you.

CHAPTER 19

The Power of Prayer

Prayer has always been a part of magick, and can be a very powerful tool. Prayer takes one of two forms; it is either an entreaty or request for divine aid, or a giving of thanks to the divine. The former of these is basically the same as a hymn, which is generally a request for divine blessing. Effective prayer requires focus and passion.

Consideration of the *Psalms* makes the intensity required for prayer plainly obvious, e.g. *"With my whole heart have I sought thee."*[45]

The emphasis can be seen on the intensity of prayer, the focusing of the entire being on the prayer. Likewise the implication is that prayer ascends from below to above, and the resulting blessing descends from above to below, echoing the hermetic formula of *"As above, so below."* This then indicates the role of the person praying as the vessel for the results of the prayer to act through. The practice of praying Qabalistically was described by Rabbi Joseph Gikatalia (1248-1305) in his classic work *The Gates of Light*:

> *"When a person prays, he must concentrate and ascend from Sephira to Sephira, from desire to desire. He must continue in this manner until in his heart he reaches the Source of the Highest Will, which is called the Infinite [Ain Soph]."*[46]

---

[45] *Psalm 119:10.*

[46] *Shaarey Orah* (The Gates of Light), Rabbi Joseph Gikatalia.

Prayer was perceived as a form of meditation, which is significant as it emphasises the need for stilling the mind and concentrating fully on the prayer. This is beautifully illustrated in a thirteenth century piece by Rabbi Jacob ben Asher (1269-1343):

> "It is taught that when one prays, he must concentrate his heart ... This means that one must concentrate fully on the words that are expressed with his lips. One must have in mind that the Divine Presence is before him, as it is written. 'I have placed God before me at all times.' [Psalm 16:8] One must arouse his concentration and banish all disturbing thoughts, so that his thoughts and intentions in prayer should be pure."[47]

Extremely useful and pertinent advice is also given in Qabalistic texts about dryness, the tendency to feel unfocused or uncomfortable or unwilling to pray.

> "There are times when you feel that you cannot pray. Do not give up even trying that day. Instead strengthen yourself all the more, and arouse your awe of God ... The same is true when you cannot pray with devotion. You should know that the King is there and you are encountering his additional guards. The only reason why you cannot come close to the King is because of this great protection surrounding Him. You must therefore fortify yourself with reverence, great strength, and additional intensity in order and come close to God. If you are successful, you will then be able to pray with the greatest possible feeling."[48]

Rabbi Abraham Abulafia (1240-95 CE), has left few surviving documents, but in one of these, *Sepher Chaije Olam Ha-Ba*, he outlines the procedure for prayer, giving an ideal framework for the modern Qabalist.

> "Prepare thyself to direct thy heart to God alone! Purify the body and retire to a lonely place ... Thou canst carry out thy purpose in thy chamber during the day, but it is better to do so at night. Withhold all

---

[47] *Tur*, Rabbi Jacob ben Asher

[48] *Likutey Yekarim 63*, Tzavaat HiRivash 72.

thy thoughts from the vanities of the world, for thou art to speak to thy Maker and crave, verily, that He will reveal to thee His power. Wrap thy prayer shawl [tallith] around thee! Bind thy phylacteries [tephillin] to head and hand, that thou mayest approach with reverence the Shekinah, with which thou must converse. Clean thy clothing, attiring thyself if possible only in white garments. If it is night, do thou kindle many lights ... Unite thy thoughts with the Divine Names and with the Angels of God, whom thou mayst think of as surrounding thee in human form."[49]

All of this makes good sense, and can be summarized as:

- Prayer is better conducted at night
- Pray by yourself in a room set aside for the purpose (i.e. temple space)
- Bathe first and wear clean white garments
- Have many candles burning in your space
- Begin with meditation
- Using the Divine Names as you move up the Tree to signify the upward ascent of the prayer to the divine.

---

[49] *Sepher Chaije Olam Ha-ba (Book of Life of the World to Come)*, Abraham Abulafia.

CHAPTER 20

Kerubic Prayer Formula

We created the Kerubic Prayer Formula as a daily sequence for bringing the essence of the Qabalah more into your life, and increasing your focus on your personal connection to the external and internal divine. It follows the traditional practice of praying three times a day, drawing on *Psalms* and the *Zohar* for inspiration. From *Psalms* comes the reference to three prayers a day, where David says *"Evening, and morning, and at noon, do I meditate, and moan."*[50] Additionally we drew on the verse, *"I recall my melody at night, I meditate with my heart, and my spirit seeks."*[51]

The *Zohar* links prayers at different times of day to specific archangels who take the prayer to the presence of God. Thus:

> *"When he opens his mouth to utter the evening prayer an eagle comes down on the weekdays to take up on its wings the evening prayer. This is the angel called Nuriel when coming from the side of Chesed and Uriel when coming from the side of Geburah, because it is a burning fire. For the morning prayer also a lion comes down to receive it in his winged arms: this is Michael. For the afternoon prayer an ox comes down to take it with his arms and horns: this is Gabriel."*[52]

The *Zohar* states that all prayers are received by the Shekinah, who weaves them into a crown which she places on God's head. This is

---

[50] *Psalm 55:18.*

[51] *Psalm 77:7.*

[52] *Zohar 23a.*

alluded to in *Proverbs* by the verse *"Blessings upon the head of the Just One."*[53] There is a clear logic in this, as we are all said to contain a spark of the Exiled Shekinah, and prayer is addressed to the divine, of whom the Greater Shekinah is part. Thus the Kerubic Prayer Formula is making use of the principle of *'As Above, So Below'*, by addressing the prayer from the divine below (Exiled Shekinah) to the divine above (Greater Shekinah). This is expressed by the great medieval Qabalist Abraham Abulafia when he wrote:

> *"Yod bears witness to the Throne that is the height of Heh, up to the height of the Vav .... And the final Heh is Shekinah's seal, the inspiration offering prophecy and salvation to all souls by her Voice and lightness."*[54]

The symbolic references here are to the Qabalistic associations of the letters of the Tetragrammaton. Yod represents the Sephira of Chokmah, bearing witness to the Throne, which is the Sephira of Binah, represented by the first Heh, and also symbolising the Greater Shekinah. The Vav here represents the Sephiroth of Construction, i.e. the six Sephiroth from Chesed to Yesod, and the final Heh is the Sephira of Malkuth and the Exiled Shekinah.

The Formula ends with the list of Divine Names which makes up the 33-fold Name of God, as found in the *Torah*. This Name is said to open the gates of prayer. All three parts of the Kerubic Prayer Formula should be performed in a day, and the practice may be continued for as long a period as you desire.

---

[53] *Proverbs* 10:6.

[54] *Sepher Ha-Ot* (*The Book of the Letter*), Abulafia.

Morning

I recall the divine song
Jahveh
I meditate with my heart
I seek with my spirit
And I speak with truth
Michael receive my morning prayer
And lift it on leonine wings
To the presence of the Shekinah
To be woven into the crown of glory
Eheieh, Yah, Yahveh, Adonai, El, Eloah, Elohim, Shaddai, Tzavaot

Noon

I recall the divine song
Jahveh
I meditate with my heart
I seek with my spirit
And I speak with truth
Gabriel receive my noon prayer
And lift it on bovine wings
To the presence of the Shekinah
To be woven into the crown of glory
Eheieh, Yah, Yahveh, Adonai, El, Eloah, Elohim, Shaddai, Tzavaot

Evening

I recall the divine song
Jahveh
I meditate with my heart
I seek with my spirit
And I speak with truth
Uriel receive my evening prayer
And lift it on aquiline wings
To the presence of the Shekinah
To be woven into the crown of glory
Eheieh, Yah, Yahveh, Adonai, El, Eloah, Elohim, Shaddai, Tzavaot

CHAPTER 21

Ruach haQadosh

"Human souls are also bound to higher levels, and therefore, when a perfect individual becomes involved in meditation upon wisdom, it is possible for him to predict future events."[55]

One of the most important spiritual developments that can be achieved through practicing Qabalah is the power of prophecy (precognition). The *Torah* is full of references and hints regarding this, which indicate how to achieve this ability, or state, which is known as Ruach HaQadosh, the *'Spirit of Holiness'*.

This is referred to explicitly in *Psalm 51:12-13*, where it says:

"A pure heart, create for me, O God,
A proper spirit, renew in me.
Cast me not away from Your presence,
And take not Your Spirit of Holiness [Ruach HaQadosh] from me."

Significantly the prophet Elijah taught that Ruach HaQadosh was available to and accessible by any person, which is obviously a perspective appreciated by modern Qabalists. Elijah said:

"I call heaven and earth to witness that any person, Jew or Gentile, man or woman, freeman or slave, if his deeds are worthy, then Ruach HaQadosh will descend upon him."[56]

---

[55] Hai Gaon (939-1038 CE).

[56] *Tan DeBei Eliahu 9.*

Eighteen of the Psalms were used as a means of attaining the state of Ruach HaQadosh, as a focus for contemplation. These are indicated by having the phrase 'A Psalm of David' in the opening verse, and are Psalms 3, 4, 5, 6, 8, 9, 12, 15, 22, 23, 29, 38, 39, 62, 63, 65, 141 & 143.

Significantly two of these Psalms begin by referring to music, indicating this was used as an aid to prophecy. Thus we see reference to string music in *Psalms 4* and *6*. This is also indicated in *2 Kings 3:15* where Elisha prophesies after a musician plays, *"Now bring me a musician. And it was when the musician played, that the hand of God came upon him."*

This is indicated even more explicitly in *1 Samuel 10:5-6*, where it says, *"You shall meet a band of prophets, coming from a high place with harp, drum, flute and lyre, and they will be prophesying. And the spirit of the Lord will come mightily upon thee, and thou shalt prophesy with them."* This is also mentioned in *1 Chronicles 25:1*, *"Who would prophesy with the harp, lute and cymbal."*

Music can strongly influence the emotions, and help create a serene state ideal for meditation. The use of instrumental music, without lyrics (there is no reference to singing) is thus a precursor that can be used to help achieve the state of Ruach HaQadosh. Rabbi Moses Maimonides explains this in his writings, saying, *"A prophet cannot prophesy at will. He concentrates his mind, sitting in a good, joyous mood and meditating. One cannot attain prophecy when he is depressed and languid, but only when he is in a joyous state. When they were seeking prophecy, the prophets would therefore have people play music for them."*[57]

The prominent modern Kabbalist Aryeh Kaplan discussed the requirements for achieving prophecy, stating that it is a step-by-step process requiring thorough mastery, using disciplines including meditation, reciting Divine Names, and praising God with prayers

---

[57] Yad, *Yesodey HaTorah* 7:4, Rabbi Moses Maimonides.

containing the Divine names. Attachment to God and continual purification are also required. Ruach HaQadosh is not an easy achievement and requires great devotion and dedication.

Another consideration which then arises is what type of meditation should you perform? The descriptions in the *Torah* suggest void meditation, removing all awareness of the body. This is indicated in Psalm 73:25-6, *"With you, I have no desire on earth. My flesh and heart fade away, God becomes the Rock of my heart and my portion forever."*[58]

Timing is also considered important, with night and dusk being the best time to meditate. Thus we see, *"Mine eyes forestalled the night-watches, that I might meditate in Thy word,"*[59]and *"Rise, meditate in the night, at the beginning of the watches."*[60]

Perhaps the best description was given by Rabbi Jacob ben Asher (1270-1343 CE), who wrote:

> *"One must concentrate on the words that leave his lips, depicting the Divine Presence right in front of him, as it is written, 'I have placed God before me at all times' [Psalms 16:8]. He must arouse his concentration, removing all disturbing thoughts so that his mind and concentration in prayer remain pure."*[61]

Another sound associated with prophecy is humming. As has already been noted, the letter Mem is associated with humming, as the water of Chokmah (the heavenly, living water) at the head of the Pillar of Water. This association is described in the book of *Job*, with another fine description of the experience of Ruach Ha Qadosh:

> *"A word was stolen to me*
> *My ear caught a touch of it*
> *In meditations from night visions*
> *When a trance falls on man*

---

[58] *Psalm 73:25-26.*

[59] *Psalm 119:48.*

[60] *Lamentations 2:19.*

[61] *Tur*, Orach Chain, 98, Rabbi Jacob ben Asher.

Terror called me and I shuddered
It terrorized most of my bones
A spirit passed before my face
Made the hair of my flesh stand on end
It stood and I did not recognise its vision
A picture was before my eyes
I heard a hum and a voice. "[62]

The Talmud also describes the ten steps which lead to Ruach HaQadosh, as an alternative to the practices previously described. These steps are:

1. Study [Malkuth]
2. Carefulness [Yesod]
3. Diligence [Hod]
4. Cleanliness [Netzach]
5. Abstention [Tiphereth]
6. Purity [Geburah]
7. Piety [Chesed]
8. Humility [Binah]
9. Fear of Sin [Chokmah]
10. Holiness [Kether]

So laid out amongst these texts we have sufficient information to give a sequence of actions to help cultivate Ruach HaQadosh in the practitioner. A final quote illustrates the following points.

> *"I recall my melody at night, I meditate with my heart, and my spirit seeks."* [63]

Cultivating the qualities listed above is a good move, for any spiritual work not just this. Meditating on a daily basis, preferably at

---

[62] *Job 4:12-16.*

[63] *Psalms 77:7.*

night, and using the divine names as mantras or prayers containing the divine names, or the appropriate psalms, will greatly benefit your spiritual development. Likewise humming before reciting such prayers, or as part of meditations, may be beneficial.

When meditating, you should concentrate on awareness of only the divine presence before you, and to go completely beyond bodily awareness. Ideally the meditation should lift the awareness through the Sephiroth to the Ain Soph. Using instrumental music as a precursor to set the mood is also recommended.

Prayers for Ruach HaQadosh

Both of the following prayers may be used to begin meditations on Ruach HaQadosh. *Psalm 51:12-14.*

> *"A pure heart, create for me, O God,*
> *A proper spirit renew in me.*
> *Cast me not away from Your presence,*
> *And take not your Holy Spirit from me.*
> *Return to me the joy of Your salvation,*
> *And let a willing spirit uphold me."*

Rabbi Joseph Tzayach in the sixteenth century gave a prayer to be used whilst in the prophetic position of kneeling with your head between your legs as a precursor to prophecy. This unique prayer includes the divine names and titles for the Sephiroth working down the Tree of Life.

> *"AHIH Asher AHIH, Crown me.*
> *Yah, give me wisdom.*
> *Elohim Chaim, grant me Understanding.*
> *El, with the right hand of his Love, make me great.*
> *Elohim, from the Terror of His judgement, protect me.*
> *IHVH, with His mercy grant me Beauty.*
> *IHVH Tzavaot, watch me Forever.*
> *Elohim Tzavaot, grant me beatitude from his Splendour.*

El Chai, make His covenant my Foundation.
Adonai, open my lips and my mouth will speak of Your praise."

Meditation for Ruach HaQadosh

The Sepher Yetzirah provides a form for meditation to follow the prayer. It says:

"The Breath of the Living God
Breath from Breath
Water from Breath
Fire from Water
Up down east west north south."

This is referring specifically to the Ruach HaQadosh (Breath of the Living God), and the creation of the three Father Letters from the three Mother Letters. Breath from breath is Aleph, water from breath is Mem coming from Aleph, and fire from water is Shin coming from Mme. The directions then refers to the permutations of Yod, Heh and Vav, which are born from Aleph, Mem and Shin. The three Mother Letters also imply the states to be overcome in achieving a suitable meditative state (see earlier chapter on The Three Mother Letters).

So after having achieved a state of calm and balance, begin by seeing the letters Aleph, Mem and Shin (from right to left), burning in flashing fire on a black background. Next transform the Aleph into Vav, then Mem into Yod, and Shin into Heh. These three Father Letters should now have replaced the Three Mothers and be hanging in flashing fire on the black background.

Now rearrange the letters, moving them so that they are in he sequence Yod Heh Vav, and see them moving to be above you, lying on the horizontal plane so that as you look upward you see them above you. See the letters hanging there, where they remain. See a second set of the letters descending towards you, and as they move below you, permutate the letters so they form the sequence Heh Yod Vav.

This sequence of fiery letters hangs in space beneath you, and sends forth another set of the sequence of letters rises up and moves to the east in front of you, permutating to the sequence Vav Yod Heh. These letters hang in front of you back in the original position you first saw the letters in.

Now see the sequence of letters give forth another set of letters which shoot through you to behind you, and then permutate to form the sequence Vav Heh Yod. Again the fiery letters hang in space, behind you. These give forth another set of letters which moves to your right, and permutates into Yod Vav Heh.

From this set of fiery letters to your right see them give forth another set of letters which move across to your left and permutate into the sequence Heh Vav Yod. You are now surrounded by the seals of God.

Conclusion

The sequence for cultivating Ruach HaQadosh is thus as follows:

- Bathe.
- Play suitable instrumental music for the mood.
- Hum for a period of several minutes.
- Perform the Kerubic Prayer Formula for the time of day
- Perform Unification up the Tree
- Perform the prayers from Psalms and Rabbi Tzayach
- Perform the meditation.

APPENDIXES

Deities of the Sephiroth

Malkuth

Deity	Function
Celtic (Gallic)	
Abellio	God of apple trees
Cernunnos	Horned God and Lord of the Beasts and the Forests
Epona	Fertility Goddess and Goddess of Horses
Sucellus	God of Forests and Agriculture
Celtic (Irish)	
Boann	Fertility Goddess, with the white cow as her symbol
Daghda	Earth God, with his cauldron of rebirth and consumption of vast quantities of porridge (oats)
Celtic (Welsh)	
Amaethon	God of agriculture
Ceridwen	Earth Goddess, with her cauldron and herb craft
Egyptian	
Geb	Earth God, his body being the Earth
Greek	
Demeter	Goddess of the fertility of the Earth and growth of vegetation
Gaia	Earth Goddess, representing the whole of the Earth
Hestia	Virgin Goddess of the Hearth
Pan	God of the Woodland and the fertilising principle
Persephone	Maiden and Bride
Roman	
Ceres	Earth Goddess linked with corn and the harvest
Fauna & Faunus	Pair of deities associated with woodlands and fertility and growth
Ops	Goddess of the Wealth of the Earth
Pomona	Goddess of Apples and Orchards
Proserpine	Earth Goddess and also as the Maiden and Bride
Terra Mater	Literally the Earth Mother
Vesta	Virgin Goddess of the Hearth
Sumerian	
Abu	Vegetation God
Ashnan	Grain Goddess
Ki (Urash)	Primal Earth Goddess

Yesod

Deity	Function
Celtic (Gallic)	
Arduinna	Lunar Goddess
Nantosuelta	Goddess of Rivers
Celtic (Welsh)	
Arianrhod	Goddess of the Silver Wheel
Rhiannon	Goddess of the Fairy Realms
Egyptian	
Khonsu	Lunar God
Thoth	As a Lunar Deity
Greek	
Artemis	Goddess of the New Moon
Hekate	Goddess of the Moon, of crossroads, and of the liminal
Morpheus	God of Dreams
Selene	Lunar Goddess
Roman	
Diana	Goddess of the New Moon
Luna	Lunar Goddess
Sumerian	
Nanna	Lunar God
Ningal	Lunar Goddess

Hod

Deity	Function
Celtic (Gallic)	
Ogmios	God of Eloquence and Writing
Celtic (Irish)	
Bride	Goddess of Healing, Smithing, Poetry and Crafts
Goibniu	Smith God and Maker of Divine Beer
Nuada	God of Healing, Writing and Magick
Ogma	God of Eloquence and Writing
Celtic (Welsh)	
Govannon	Smith God and Maker of Divine Beer
Gwydion	Magician God
Math Mathonwy	God of Sorcery
Nudd/Nodens	God of Healing, Writing and Magick
Egyptian	
Anubis	Psychopomp and God of Perfumery
Seshat	Goddess of Writing
Shu	Air God

Greek	
Asclepius	God of Healing
Hermes	God of Magick, Communication and Healing, and as Psychopomp and Trickster
Iris	Messenger Goddess bearing the Caduceus, and also of the Rainbow, hinting at Paroketh
Roman	
Mercury	God of Magick and Messenger
Sumerian	
Enlil	Air God
Nibada	Goddess of Learning
Ninlil	Air Goddess

Netzach

Deity	Function
Celtic (Irish)	
Aine	Goddess of Love and Fertility
Morrigan	Goddess of Sex and battle, also the raven is one of her aspects (the Badb)
Celtic (Welsh)	
Branwen	Goddess of Beauty and Love
Egyptian	
Bastet	Goddess of Pleasure
Bes	Protective Warrior God associated with love, marriage and childbirth
Hathor	Goddess of sensuality, sexuality, and dance
Sebek	God of Fertility and protection
Greek	
Aphrodite	Goddess of Love, often inciting lust and battle
Nike	Goddess of Victory, the name of the Sephira
Roman	
Lucifer	The Morning Star
Venus	Goddess of Love and Gardens
Sumerian	
Inanna	Goddess of Love and War, and representing the morning star

Tiphereth

Deity	Function
Celtic (British)	
Belenus	Sun God and Lord of Light
Maponus	Child of Promise who brings Health or Sickness to the Land
Sulis	Solar Goddess
Celtic (Irish)	
Bile	Sun God and Lord of Light
Lugh	Lord of Light
Mog Ruith	Sun God in his bronze chariot flying through the sky
Celtic (Welsh)	
Beli	Sun God and Lord of Light
Gwyn Ap Nudd	Lord of Light and Ruler of the Otherworld
Lleu	Lord of Light
Mabon	Child of Promise who brings Health or Sickness to the Land
Egyptian	
Horus	Conquering Solar Child
Nefertem	Child of the Dawn
Osiris	Sacrificed God
Ra	Solar God
Sekhmet	Fierce midday sun and manifestation of Re's wrath
Greek	
Apollo	Lord of Light, Prophecy and Music
Dionysus	The Liberator
Eos	Goddess of the Dawn
Helios	Solar God
Roman	
Aurora	Goddess of the Dawn
Sol Invictus	Conquering Sun
Sumerian	
Dumuzi	Dying and Resurrected God
Utu	Solar God

Geburah

Deity	Function
Celtic (British)	
Andraste	War Goddess
Morrigan	War Goddess
Egyptian	
Horus	As War God
Seth	God of violent forces, and the sacredness of red to him as a colour of power and danger
Greek	
Ares	War God
Eris	Goddess of Discord, unbalanced Martial energy
Nemesis	Goddess of Divine Retribution
Roman	
Bellona	War Goddess
Discordia	Goddess of Discord who preceded Mars' chariot into battle
Mars	War God
Sumerian	
Inanna	As War Goddess

Chesed

Deity	Function
Celtic (Gallic)	
Taranis	As the "Thunderer", God of Storms
Egyptian	
Amun	Ruler of the Gods
Greek	
Themis	Goddess of Justice
Zeus	Ruler of the Gods
Roman	
Jupiter	Ruler of the Gods
Justitia	Goddess of Justice
Sumerian	
An	Sky God

Daath

Deity	Function
Egyptian	
Apep	The chaos serpent, as challenging the sun god Re (Tiphereth)
Heka	Lord of Ka's (souls) and being the primal force of magick
Khephri	As the beetle God pushing the sun in a dung ball through the blackness
Serket	Scorpion Goddess, as "she who causes the throat to breathe"
Set	As a Chaos Deity
Greek	
Erebus	The Primordial Darkness fathering Hypnos (Sleep) and Thanatos (Death)
Prometheus	Benefactor of mankind, stealing the fire from heaven
Roman	
Janus	Two-faced God looking down to the physical and up to the ethereal
Sumerian	
Tiamat	Goddess of the Primal Waters of Chaos

Binah

Deity	Function
Celtic (Irish)	
Cailleach	Sterile Mother aspect of the Goddess
Danu	Mother of the Gods and Goddess of Wisdom
Celtic (Welsh)	
Don	Mother of the Gods and Goddess of Wisdom
Egyptian	
Heket	Divine midwife at the primeval creation
Isis	Mother Goddess, and by her name meaning throne
Mut	Wife of Amun and Primal Mother
Neith	Primal Goddess who gives birth to Re and Apep
Nephthys	Dark Fertile Mother
Sia	As perception, forming a triad with Hu and Re
Tefnut	Goddess of the waters and Eye of Re
Greek	
Cybele	Dark Mother who wields the sickle
Hera	Queen of the Gods

Rhea	Partner of Kronos and mother of the Titans
Tethys	Sea Goddess embodying the Great Sea (Marah)
Roman	
Fortuna	Goddess of Fate
Juno	Queen of the Gods
Sumerian	
Nammu	Goddess of the watery deep

Chokmah

Deity	Function
Celtic (Irish)	
Lir	Sea God
Mannanan Mac Lir	God of Magick and the Sea
Celtic (Welsh)	
Bran	Wise Oracle and Severed Head
Manawydan	Sea God
Egyptian	
Atum	Speaker of the logos and first from the primal waters
Hu	As the magical power of words and as "he who spoke in the darkness"
Khnum	Creator God giving form
Nuit	The Cosmos
Greek	
Athena	Goddess of Wisdom, sprung from her father's head
Metis	Goddess of Wisdom
Poseidon	Sea God
Roman	
Coelus	God of the Sky and the Heavens
Janus	Twin-faced God of Time, looking forward and backwards, and representing duality
Minerva	Goddess of Wisdom, sprung from her father's head
Neptune	Sea God
Sumerian	
An	God of the Heavens
Enki	Goddess of Wisdom and Magick

Kether

Deity	Function
Egyptian	
Amun	Creator God, forming order from the primaeval chaos
Ptah	Creator God who brings the universe into being through the "thoughts of his heart and the words of his mouth"
Ra	Creator God, bringing the universe into being
Greek	
Aether	First manifestation of Deity from the endlessness of Nox, referred to as the place from whence all souls emanate
Ananke	Goddess of destiny and Mother of the Fates
Zeus Hypsistos	The ultimate deity, of whom all others are perceived as aspects
Roman	
Theos Hypsistos	The ultimate deity, of whom all others are perceived as aspects
Sumerian	
Apsu	God of the Sweet Waters of Creation

APPENDIX 2

Reincarnation & the Qabalah

The idea of reincarnation, or transmigration of souls, known as 'gilgul' (meaning *revolving* or *swirling*) was one that became integrated into Qabalistic belief, being first published in the *Bahir* in the late thirteenth century CE. On death the parts of the soul all go to their appointed places. The *Nephesh* sinks into the earth, to go to *Gehinnom* (hell) if the person has been bad, the Ruach stays with the body, and the *Neshamah* ascends to the Throne of God, where the Throne sustains it until it is ready to descend back into physical form.

This doctrine is hinted at by the name of the heaven of Kether, i.e. *Rashith ha-Gilgalim* ('*the first swirlings*'), coming from the same root as the word *gilgul*. The soul aspires to its highest aspect, the *Yechidah*, seeking to elevate the lower aspects so they may be united with the highest and then re-merge with the ultimate divine.

There are a number of variants of this belief, such as where the souls go depending on conduct. A soul that has fulfilled its spiritual destiny does not need to continue reincarnating, and is said to be stored in holiness by God until the end of time, when it is rejoined with its body (*Guph*), its *Ruach* and its *Nephesh*. God will then cause dew (which is the divine light) to exude from His head that will flow through the Sephiroth until it reaches the earth. The dew is said to be that which would have caused Adam and Eve to have become immortal, and will enable the resurrected soul to be remerged with the primal Adam.

When all the souls have remerged with Adam, he can be restored to his state of grace from before the Fall and exile. In this way every person is part of the process of restoration, '*tikkun*'.

A soul that has knowingly perpetrated evil will return to a lesser form, such as an animal, plant or even stone. This doctrine is analogous to the Hindu concept of karmic reincarnation, and is thought to have its roots in Platonic and Neo-Platonic philosophies. This is made even clearer in the *Zohar*, which raises the issue of reincarnation in an interesting manner, with discussion of the final judgement. It says:

> "Said Rabbi Hizkiah: 'If it be so that all the dead bodies will rise up from the dust, what will happen to a number of bodies which shared in succession the same soul?' Rabbi Jose answered: ' Those bodies which were unworthy and did not achieve their purpose will be regarded as though they had not been: as they were a withered tree in this world, so will they be regarded at the time of the resurrection. Only the last that had been firmly planted and took root and prospered will come to life, as it says, 'For he shall be as a tree planted by the waters ... but its foliage shall be luxuriant (Jer 17:8).'"[64]

A later version of this doctrine changed the concept of rebirth until perfection is reached with a cycle of only four incarnations. If by the end of the fourth life the soul had not reached a basic level of development it would roam the earth as a spirit (called a *dybbuk*) that sought to possess other people to control their bodies and be returned to the flesh. If the soul did reach a level of attainment it would find sanctuary until the day of restitution.

The idea of reincarnation is hinted at in earlier texts, such as in *3 Enoch*, where it describes the vision of, *"the souls of the righteous who have already been created and have returned, and the souls of the righteous who have not yet been created."* A clear reincarnation reference indeed! Thus we can see that it was not just the influence of Neo-Platonism which produced a doctrine of reincarnation in Qabalah.

---

[64] *Zohar 1.131a.*

Attributions of the Paths

Path	Joins	Letter	English	Meaning	No.	Colour
11	1-2	Aleph	A	Ox	1	Bright Yellow
12	1-3	Beth	B	House	2	Orange
13	1-6	Gimel	G	Camel	3	Violet
14	2-3	Daleth	D	Door	4	Emerald Green
15	2-6	Heh	H, E, A	Window	5	Red
16	2-4	Vav	V, U, O	Nail	6	Red-Orange
17	3-6	Zain	Z	Sword	7	Orange
18	3-5	Cheth	Ch	Fence	8	Orange-Yellow
19	4-5	Teth	T	Serpent	9	Yellow
20	4-6	Yod	I, Y	Hand	10	Yellow-Green
21	4-7	Kaph	K	Palm	20	Royal Blue
22	5-6	Lamed	L	Ox-Goad	30	Green
23	5-8	Mem	M	Water	40	Deep Blue
24	6-7	Nun	N	Fish	50	Green-Blue
25	6-9	Samekh	S	Prop	60	Blue
26	6-8	Ayin	O, Aa, Ngh	Eye	70	Blue-Violet
27	7-8	Peh	P, Ph	Mouth	80	Scarlet Red
28	7-9	Tzaddi	Tz	Fish-hook	90	Violet
29	7-10	Qoph	Q	Back of Head	100	Violet-Red
30	8-9	Resh	R	Head	200	Yellow
31	8-10	Shin	Sh	Tooth	300	Glowing Red
32	9-10	Tav	Th	Cross	400	Indigo

Planetary Hours

The planetary hours are not the same as the sixty-minute hours beginning at midnight that we use for normal timekeeping. The planetary days are divided into twenty-four planetary hours, which run from sunrise to sunrise of the next planetary day.

The period of daylight from sunrise to sunset is divided into the twelve 'hours' of the day, and the period of darkness extending from sunset to sunrise of the next day is divided into twelve 'hours' of night. Combined these give the twenty-four hours of the planetary day.

As the duration of daylight and darkness in a day will always be different (except at the Spring and Autumn Equinoxes), the planetary hours are sometimes called the unequal hours. Almanacs, ephemeredes and the internet are all sources you can use to discover the sunrise and sunset times, enabling you to calculate the planetary hours.

Planetary Hours of the Day

Hour	Sunday	Monday	Tuesday	Wednesday	Thursday	Friday	Saturday
1	Sun	Moon	Mars	Mercury	Jupiter	Venus	Saturn
2	Venus	Saturn	Sun	Moon	Mars	Mercury	Jupiter
3	Mercury	Jupiter	Venus	Saturn	Sun	Moon	Mars
4	Moon	Mars	Mercury	Jupiter	Venus	Saturn	Sun
5	Saturn	Sun	Moon	Mars	Mercury	Jupiter	Venus
6	Jupiter	Venus	Saturn	Sun	Moon	Mars	Mercury
7	Mars	Mercury	Jupiter	Venus	Saturn	Sun	Moon
8	Sun	Moon	Mars	Mercury	Jupiter	Venus	Saturn
9	Venus	Saturn	Sun	Moon	Mars	Mercury	Jupiter
10	Mercury	Jupiter	Venus	Saturn	Sun	Moon	Mars
11	Moon	Mars	Mercury	Jupiter	Venus	Saturn	Sun
12	Saturn	Sun	Moon	Mars	Mercury	Jupiter	Venus

Planetary Hours of the Night

Hour	Sunday	Monday	Tuesday	Wednesday	Thursday	Friday	Saturday
1	Jupiter	Venus	Saturn	Sun	Moon	Mars	Mercury
2	Mars	Mercury	Jupiter	Venus	Saturn	Sun	Moon
3	Sun	Moon	Mars	Mercury	Jupiter	Venus	Saturn
4	Venus	Saturn	Sun	Moon	Mars	Mercury	Jupiter
5	Mercury	Jupiter	Venus	Saturn	Sun	Moon	Mars
6	Moon	Mars	Mercury	Jupiter	Venus	Saturn	Sun
7	Saturn	Sun	Moon	Mars	Mercury	Jupiter	Venus
8	Jupiter	Venus	Saturn	Sun	Moon	Mars	Mercury
9	Mars	Mercury	Jupiter	Venus	Saturn	Sun	Moon
10	Sun	Moon	Mars	Mercury	Jupiter	Venus	Saturn
11	Venus	Saturn	Sun	Moon	Mars	Mercury	Jupiter
12	Mercury	Jupiter	Venus	Saturn	Sun	Moon	Mars

Formula:

The method of calculating these hours is straightforward if you apply the simple formula used to calculate the hours.

- Add together the number of hours and minutes from sunrise (SR) to sunset (SS) on the required day.
- Convert this into minutes, giving a total period of daylight, which we shall call D.
- Divide D by 12 to give the length of a planetary hour, H.
- To work out when the appropriate planetary hours begin on the day you wish to work, simply add the number of the hour (N) minus one, e.g. the third hour begins after two (3-1) hours have passed.
- Thus the formula for when the hour starts is SR + (N-1) * D, and the hour then runs for D minutes, ending at SR + N * D.
- The same procedure is used for night hours, but taking SS as the base point to start from rather than sunrise.

Example:

- Let us say sunrise (SR) is at 6.30am and sunset (SS) is at 8.42pm
- The period of time between these two times is 14 hours and 10 minutes, which equals 14 * 60 + 12 = 852
- So D = 850, and the length of a planetary hour H, will be 852/12 = 71 minutes
- You have decided to perform your ceremony on the eighth hour of the day, as being more suitable, so N = 8.
- The ceremony will then begin at SR + (N-1) * D, which in this instance is 6.30 + 7 * 71 = 6.30 + 497 minutes = 6.30 + 8 hours and 17 minutes = 2.47pm.
- The hour runs from 2.47pm for 71 minutes, ending at 3.58pm.

APPENDIX 5

Incense

Incense and anointing oil stimulate the sense of smell (and hence memory), which plays a significant part in ceremonies. This fact was well known to the early Qabalists, and many early texts, including those in the Bible, make reference to the aromatic ingredients used in incenses. Thus in *Psalms 141:2* we see, *"Let my prayer be set forth as incense before thee."*

In *Exodus 30:33 & 30:38* there are specific instructions regarding the use of incense. Thus *"Aaron shall burn thereon incense of sweet spices"*, and *"Ye shall offer no strange incense thereon."* This is clearly an injunction to use specific recipes for worship and no other.

The burning of incense can be seen as an ascent of the tree of Life, taking the scent from the physical to the subtle, from visible to invisible, carrying prayers and intent on the sweet fragrances to the heavens.

The Biblical recipes for incense and anointing oil are ideal for Qabalistic ceremonies, as they are both multi-purpose. The Holy Incense recipe is one for consecration and sanctification.

Holy Incense

"Take unto thee sweet spices, storax, and onycha, and galbanum; sweet spices with pure frankincense; of each there shall be a like weight and thou shalt make of it incense, a perfume after the art of the perfumer, seasoned with salt, pure and holy."[65]

There is a query on one ingredient here. The word which onycha is translated from is *shecheleth*, meaning *'nail/claw'*. This term was also

---

[65] *Exodus 30:34-35.*

sometimes applied to cloves, so this could be used rather than onycha which is made from ground-up molluscs.

Recipe

1 part storax

1 part onycha (or clove)

1 part galbanum

1 part frankincense

Pinch sea salt

Holy Anointing Oil

The recipe for anointing oil is given in *Exodus 30:23-5*, along with instructions for anointing all the objects in the temple with it, including the participants.　As this recipe uses resins, it needs to infuse for a decent period of time. We suggest 26 weeks, as a suitable duration. We have converted the units into modern ones. Although the quantities are large, they could be scaled down appropriately to a smaller quantity. Of course with such a long infusion time, it is worth making a decent quantity so that you don't run out!

Recipe

575g myrrh

287.5g cinnamon

287.5g sweet Calamus

575g cassia

1L olive oil

Gematria

The esoteric meanings of scripture and other texts, which are developed through the techniques of Gematria, Notariqon and Temurah, have become a major part of modern Qabalah. As these practices are frequently used for meditation and inspiration, we have included a précis of their use as an appendix for those who wish to explore them further, or include them in their practices.

Gematria

As every Hebrew letter has a number attributed to it, it follows that every word in Hebrew has a numerical value, given by adding the numbers attributed to its component letters. Gematria is simply the comparison of words whose constituent letters create the same total. E.g. *Unity (AChD)* and *Love (AHBH)* both add to 13, and we can say from this that the nature of unity is love, or love promotes unity.

Gematria encourages you to develop your intuition by looking at possible links between words with the same numerical total. However these links should leap from your mind, rather than be a long tortuous process of trying to make things fit. When Gematria causes you to make a connection, it is often like a little lightning flash of inspiration which gives you a moment of realisation or insight.

Notariqon

Notariqon comes from the Latin *notarius* meaning *'shorthand writer'.* Notariqon is the creation of a word by taking the first letters of a sentence and forming them together, i.e. an acronym. E.g. AGLA is Notariqon of *Ateh Gibor Le-olahm Adonai ('To Thee O Lord the Glory to the*

Ages'), and the prayer ending of Amen which is used throughout Christianity is Notariqon of *Al Mlk Natz* ('*The Lord and faithful King*').

This technique is also sometimes applied by taking the first and last letter of each word to form the new words. So if we took the phrase *Chokmah Nistorah* ('*Secret Wisdom*', a name ascribed to Qabalah), the first letters give us *chen* (ChN) meaning '*grace*' and the last letters give us *Heh* spelt in full (HH), meaning '*window*'. So from this we could say that secret wisdom is the window to grace.

Notariqon can also be applied as an expansive principle rather than a contractive one. In this instance a word is expanded out, so that each letter in the word becomes the first letter of a word in a sentence. So e.g. Berashith, meaning '*In the beginning*', is the first word of the book of *Genesis*. In Hebrew it is written BRAShITh, which could be expanded to "*Berashith Rahi Elohim Sheyequelo Israel Torah*", meaning: "*In the Beginning the Gods saw that Israel would accept the law.*"

Temurah

Temurah is the name given to transposition of the letters of the Hebrew alphabet, so that each letter is consistently replaced by another one, given by the particular cipher used. By this means different words are created. Temurah was used largely in the making of talismans. There are many different forms of Temurah, of which those below are the best known and easiest to work.

The Atbash Cipher, is where the letters are reversed (so Aleph is replaced by Tav, Beth by Shin ... Shin by Beth, Tav by Aleph). It takes its name from the first and last two letters of the alphabet and their manner of switching, thus ATBaSh (i.e. Aleph - Tav, Beth - Shin).

The Avgad Cipher, where each letter is replaced by the one following it (Aleph replaced with Beth, Beth with Gimel, etc).

Boustrophedon, is where alternate lines are written right to left and then left to right (i.e. reversed). Reading downwards then gives new words. This technique was used to form the seventy-two names in the Shemhamphorash.

Thashrag, is where the word is written backwards, e.g. AIN becomes NIA, AL becomes LA, etc.

The Tarot and the Tree of Life

The connection between the Tarot and the Tree of Life is a comparatively recent one in the history of the Qabalah. The origins of this association may be found in the works of Antoine Court de Gébelin (1719-84). He published an essay by the Comte de Mellet (in 1781) with the first known suggestion of the connection between the twenty-two Tarot Trumps and the letters of the Hebrew alphabet, and hence the Paths of the Tree.

This association has become popularised, largely due to the influence of Eliphas Levi and the Hermetic Order of the Golden Dawn. For this reason we will briefly discuss the attributions, whilst recognising that this connection has no place in the mainstream of Qabalistic Magick, particularly pre-eighteenth century.

The earliest known Tarot decks did not have the now standard set of twenty-two Trumps and fifty-six minor cards in four suits. Rather they were sets of Trump sequences, with the earliest decks having e.g. fifty Trumps, like the Mantegna deck. This deck was created by fifteenth century engraver Andrea Mantegna, a worker of *trionfi* (triumphs, a name for engraved symbolic cards).

Interestingly Mantegna and his successors were influenced by the triumphal parades of Renaissance Italy, where a series of personified images *'triumphed'*, each over the preceding personification. This sequence would then manifest as the development of the Trump sequence in the Tarot. Coincidentally this also hints at the evolutionary development of the Qabalist working systematically up the Tree of Life, building on what has been before. This coincidence may be due to the association of the *Trionfi* with the memory theatre of Camillo, which presented a system of magical memory development harking back to the ancient world.

Following on from the attribution of the Trumps to the Paths of the Tree of Life, the sequence of cards 1-10 were attributed to the Sephiroth by number, and the court cards attributed to the appropriate Sephiroth to match the *Parzufim* ('*faces*') and letters of Tetragrammaton. These associations also included matching the suits to the Four Worlds through Tetragrammaton.

Tarot by the Four Worlds

Letter	Yod	Heh	Vav	Heh
World	Atziluth	Briah	Yetzirah	Assiah
Element	Fire	Water	Air	Earth
Suit	Wands	Cups	Swords	Disks
Parzufim	Father	Mother	Son	Daughter
Court Card	King	Queen	Prince	Princess

The Minor Arcana on the Tree

Sephira	Minor Arcana	Court Cards
Kether	4 Aces	
Chokmah	4 Twos	4 Kings
Binah	4 Threes	4 Queens
Chesed	4 Fours	
Geburah	4 Fives	
Tiphereth	4 Sixes	4 Princes
Netzach	4 Sevens	
Hod	4 Eights	
Yesod	4 Nines	
Malkuth	4 Tens	4 Princesses

The Major Arcana on the Tree

Path	Trump	Letter
11	The Fool	Aleph
12	The Magician	Beth
13	The High Priestess	Gimel
14	The Empress	Daleth
15	The Emperor	Heh
16	The Hierophant	Vav
17	The Lovers	Zain
18	The Chariot	Cheth
19	Justice	Teth
20	The Hermit	Yod
21	The Wheel of Fortune	Kaph
22	Strength	Lamed
23	The Hanged Man	Mem
24	Death	Nun
25	Temperance	Samekh
26	The Devil	Ayin
27	The Tower	Peh
28	The Star	Tzaddi
29	The Moon	Qoph
30	The Sun	Resh
31	Judgement	Shin
32	The Universe	Tav

The Hebrew Alphabet

Letter	Hebrew	Meaning	English	Number	Path
Aleph	א	Ox	A	1	11
Beth	ב	House	B	2	12
Gimel	ג	Camel	G	3	13
Daleth	ד	Door	D	4	14
Heh	ה	Window	H, E, A	5	15
Vav	ו	Nail	V, U, O	6	16
Zain	ז	Sword	Z	7	17
Cheth	ח	Window	Ch	8	18
Teth	ט	Snake	T	9	19
Yod	י	Hand	I, J, Y	10	20
Kaph	כ	Palm (of hand)	K	20	21
Lamed	ל	Ox-goad	L	30	22
Mem	מ	Water	M	40	23
Nun	נ	Fish	N	50	24
Samekh	ס	Prop	S	60	25
Ayin	ע	Eye	Aa, O	70	26
Peh	פ	Mouth	P, Ph	80	27
Tzaddi	צ	Fish-hook	Tz	90	28
Qoph	ק	Back of Head	Q	100	29
Resh	ר	Head	R	200	30
Shin	ש	Tooth	Sh	300	31
Tav	ת	Cross	Th	400	32

Bibliography

Abulafia, Abraham; *Get Ha-Shemot: Divorce of the Names*; 2007; Providence University; Providence

Agrippa, Cornelius; *Three Books of Occult Philosophy*; 2005 (first published 1531-33); Llewellyn; Minnesota

Arbel, Vita Daphna; *Beholders of Divine Secrets: Mysticism and Myth in the Hekhalot and Merkavah Literature*; 2003; SUNY Press; Albany

Athanassiadi, Polymnia & Frede, Michael; *Pagan Monotheism in Late Antiquity*; 1999; Oxford University Press; Oxford

Bischoff, Erich; *Kabbala*; 1991; Red Wheel/Weiser; Maine

Blau, J.L.; *The Christian Interpretation of the Cabala in the Renaissance*; 1944; Columbia University Press; Columbia

Butler, E.M.; *Ritual Magic*; 1979; Cambridge University Press; Cambridge

Buxbaum, Yitzhak; *Jewish Spiritual Practices*; 1995; Aronson

Charles, R.H. (trans); *The Book of Enoch*; 1917; SPCK; London

Dan, Joseph; *Ancient Jewish Mysticism*; 1993; Israel MOD Publishing House; Tel Aviv

Davila, James R.; *Descenders to the Chariot: The People behind the Hekhalot Literature*; 2001; Supplements to the *Journal for the Study of Judaism*, volume 70

Dennis, Rabbi Geoffrey W.; *The Encyclopaedia of Jewish Myth, Magic and Mysticism*; 2007; Llewellyn; Minnesota

----------; *The Use of Water as a Medium for Altered States of Consciousness in Early Jewish Mysticism*; 2009; in *Anthropology of Consciousness* 19.1:84-106

Deutsch, Nathaniel; *Guardians of the Gate: Angelic Vice regency in Late Antiquity*; 1999; Brill; Leiden

Elior, Rachel; *The Three Temples: On the Emergence of Jewish Mysticism*; 2004; Littmann; Oregon

Franck, Adolphe; *The Kabbalah*; 1967; University Books; New York

Gikatilla, R. Joseph; *Sha'are Orah*; 1994; Harper Collins; London

Ginsburg, Christian D.; *The Kabbalah, its Doctrines, Development and Literature*; 1970; Routledge; London

Ginzberg, Louis; *On Jewish Law and Lore*; 1970; Atheneum; New York

Goldmerstein, L.; *Magical Sacrifice in the Jewish Kabbalah*; 1896, in *Folklore VII*

Green, Arthur; *Keter: The Crown of God in Early Jewish Mysticism*; 1997; Princeton University

Gruenwald, Ithamar; *Apocalyptic and Merkavah Mysticism*; 1980; E.J. Brill; Leiden

Idel, Moshe; *Kabbalah: New Perspectives*; 1990; Yale University Press

----------- *Hasidism: Between Ecstasy and Magic*; 1995; SUNY; New York

----------- *Studies in Ecstatic Kabbalah*; 1988; SUNY; New York

----------- *The Early Kabbalah*; 1986; Paulist Press; New York

Janowitz, Naomi; *Icons of Power: Ritual Practices in Late Antiquity*; 2002; Pennsylvania State University Press; Pennsylvania

Kanarfogel, Ephraim; *Peering through the Lattices: Mystical, Magical, and Pietistic Dimensions in the Tosafist Period*; 2000; Wayne State University Press; Detroit

Kaplan, Aryeh; *Sefer Yetzirah: The Book of Creation*; 1997; Weiser Books; Maine

-----------; *Meditation and Kabbalah*; 1982; Red Wheel/Weiser; Maine

-----------; *The Bahir Illumination*; 1979; Red Wheel/Weiser; Maine

-----------; *The Living Torah* (5 volumes); 1981; Moznaim, New York

-----------; *Jewish Meditation: A Practical Guide*; 1995; Schocken Books

Karr, Don (ed), & Smith, Morton (trans); *Hekhalot Rabbati: The Greater Treatise Concerning the Palaces of Heaven*; 2009; Don Karr

Klutz, Todd (ed); *Magic in the Biblical World: From the Rod of Aaron to the Ring of Solomon*; 2003; T&T Clark International; London

Lesses, Rebecca Macy; *Ritual Practices to Gain Power. Angels, Incantations, and Revelation in Early Jewish Mysticism*; 1997; Trinity Press International; Pennsylvania

Levertoff, Paul P. (trans); *The Zohar* (5 volumes); 1959; Bennett; New York

Levi, Eliphas; *The Book of Splendours*; 1975; Aquarian; London

-----------; *The Mysteries of the Qabalah*; 2001; Weiser; Maine

-----------; *The Magical Ritual of the Sanctum Regnum*; 1970; Crispin Press; London

----------; *Transcendental Magic*; 1995; Tiger Books International PLC; Twickenham

Luzzatto, Rabbi Moses; *General Principles of Kabbalah*; 1970; Research Centre of Kabbalah Press; New York

McLean, Adam (ed); *The Magical Calendar*; 1994 (first published 1620); Phanes Press; Michigan

---------- (ed); *A Treatise on Angel Magic*; 1982; Magnum Opus; Edinburgh

Meltzer, David; *The Secret Garden: An Anthology in the Kabbalah*; 1976; Seabury Press Inc; New York

Meyer, Marvin W., & Smith, Richard (eds); *Ancient Christian Magic: Coptic Texts of Ritual Power*; 1999; Princeton University Press; Princeton

Myer, Issac; *Qabbalah*; 1970; Stuart & Watkins; London

Padeh, Zwe & Menzi, D.W; *The Palace of Adam Kadmon*; 1999; Jason Aronson Inc; Jerusalem

Ponce, Charles; *Kabbalah*; 1974; Garnstone Press; London

Peterson, Joseph H. (ed); *The Sixth and Seventh Books of Moses: Or, Moses' Magical Spirit Art*; 2008; Ibis Press; Florida

Prinke, Rafal T.; *Mantegna's Prints in Tarot History*; 1990, in *Manteia* 4.9.

Rankine, David; *Climbing the Tree of Life*; 2005; Avalonia; London

----------; *Walking the Tree of Life*; 2007; Unpublished MS

Rankine, David, & d'Este, Sorita; *Practical Planetary Magick*; 2007; Avalonia; London

Reuchlin, Johann; *De Arte Cabalistica*; 1983; Abaris Books

Salkeld, John; *Treatise of Angels*; in Sloane MS 2594; 17th Century; British Library

Savedow, Steve (trans); *Sepher Rezial Hemelach: The Book of the Angel Rezial*; 2000; Samuel Weiser; Maine

Schäfer, Peter; *Mirror of His Beauty: Feminine Images of God from the Bible to the Early Kabbalah*; 2002; Princeton University Press; Princeton

----------; *The Hidden and Manifest God. Some Major Themes in Early Jewish Mysticism*; 1992; SUNY; New York

Scheinkin, David; *Path of Kabbalah*; 1986; Continuum International Publishing Group

Scholem, Gershom; *Jewish Gnosticism Merkavah Mysticism and Talmudic Tradition*; 1965; Jewish Theological Seminary of America; New York

-----------; *Major Trends in Jewish Mysticism*; 1969; Schocken; New York

-----------; *On the Kabbalah and Its Symbolism*; 1965; Schocken; New York

-----------; *On the Mystical Shape of the Godhead*; 1991; Schocken

-----------; *Origins of the Kabbalah*; 1990; Princeton University Press; Princeton

Schrire, Theodor; *Hebrew Amulets*; 1966; Routledge & Kegan Paul; London

Shaked, Shaul (ed); *Officina Magica: Essays on the Practice of Magic in Antiquity*; 2005; Brill; Leiden

Skinner, Stephen, and Rankine, David; *The Keys to the Gateway of Magic*; 2005; Golden Hoard Press; Singapore

Suster, Gerald; *The Truth About the Tarot*; 1991; Skoob Esoterica; London

Swartz, Michael D.; *Scholastic Magic: Ritual and Revelation in Early Jewish Mysticism*; 1996; Princeton University Press; New Jersey

-----------; *Mystical Prayer in Early Jewish Mysticism: An Analysis of Ma'aseh Merkavah*; 1992; Mohr Siebeck; Tubingen

Tishby, Isaiah & Lachower, Y.F.; *The Wisdom of the Zohar*; 1989; Oxford University Press; Oxford

Trachtenberg, Joshua; *Jewish Magic and Superstition*; 1939; Behrman House; New York

Verman, Mark; *The History and Varieties of Jewish Meditation*; 1996; Jacob Aronson Inc; New Jersey

Waite, A.E.; *The Holy Kabbalah*; 1965; University Books; New York

CPSIA information can be obtained at www.ICGtesting.com
Printed in the USA
LVOW100720261212

313226LV00006B/221/P